THE ART OF
BECOMING
WHOLE

A Guide to Self-Mastery

POOJA KHANNA

The Art Of Becoming Whole © Pooja Khanna

First Edition 2020

Cover Design by Sonal Churi

Layout and typesetting by Sonal Churi & Brand Soul Creations

TABLE OF CONTENTS

PREFACE

At some point in our lives, we find ourselves overcome with the desire to become better people—to grow, expand, and evolve. This innate desire for personal expansion can lead us down many paths as we develop within our lives. We understand that we want to be "better", we know that we want more peace and happiness in our relationships, we realize that we want to release patterns of behavior that don't serve us anymore—but we don't know how to get there.

We are all a combination of divine and human qualities. We all struggle with our flaws and triggers—in different ways, to different degrees. Becoming conscious of them allows us to reclaim our power and rewrite them to choose a new path forward for ourselves. This is the first step to *Becoming Whole*.

Becoming Whole is a lifelong project, and hence, a step-by-step effort on each aspect of our inner world yields much better results. Each chapter in this book focuses on one aspect of our inner being that needs to be brought into wholeness. It helps to shine light on our triggers and patterns—based on our ego, projections and past hurt—and the underlying beliefs and thoughts that need to be healed to bring about deep inner transformation.

I have personally experienced all the fears, insecurities, doubts, patterns and projections that I have described in this book; and have gone through an arduous personal journey to transform myself. I was an Executive for 13 years with top blue-chip companies in the US, launching businesses across the globe. I earned numerous awards and accolades, but my demanding work life—and the stress and anxiety associated with it—led me to develop a condition called adrenal fatigue, which caused me to lose all my stamina and made me dizzy all the time. With the help of a hypnotherapist, a healer, and a spiritual coach I was successful in healing myself. Meditation, journaling, affirmations, chanting, connecting with nature, and spiritual retreats became a way of life for me, ever since.

After coming back to full strength, I founded an online wellness and healing platform called *Begin to Heal*, to book sessions with hundreds of holistic wellness practitioners, spiritual coaches and healers in the United States. We were featured in premium wellness outlets and newspapers as a '*revolutionary holistic wellness platform*' within a few months of launch and I was invited to speak on panels, podcasts, and radio shows in New York. Through trials and triumph alike, *Begin to Heal* was born out of my passion to help others in their journeys to reclaim their mental and emotional wellbeing. As a huge proponent of spiritual wellness, I believe in taking accountability for our beliefs, thoughts and feelings, and the role they play in shaping our lives and our health.

As you read this book, you will begin to recognize the transformations taking place within you, bit by bit, layer by layer. You will begin to notice that you respond differently to situations. Whenever a situation arises that causes a disturbance within you, you will begin to ask yourself, "What is this situation revealing to me about me?" You will release your expectations, disappointments, and victim stories, bringing much-needed growth and peace in your life. You will develop a strong sense of self-worth, by letting go of self-limiting beliefs and the need to seek validation from others.

The ultimate goal for our souls is to find more peace and happiness in our lives, to move from self-sabotage to self-mastery; and to merge with Consciousness. This book can help you, step by step, to learn the art of becoming whole again—to grow, evolve, expand, heal, and return to your original pure, divine nature.

ACKNOWLEDGEMENTS

I am eternally grateful to GD and Amit Gaur of Core Healing India, my spiritual guides, for helping me through this process of inner transformation. They have been guiding me for over 5 years and all my deepest epiphanies and spiritual realizations have come during my sessions with them.

I acknowledge, with gratitude, the learnings from the book, *A Course in Miracles* & Access Consciousness© that I have incorporated into this book.

Warmly,
Pooja

INTRODUCTION

Nan-in, a Japanese master during the Meiji era, received a university professor who came to inquire about Zen. Nan-in served tea. He poured into his visitor's cup, until it began to overflow. The professor watched the overflow until he no longer could restrain himself and said. "It is full. No more will go in!"

Nan-in replied, "Just like this cup, you are full of your own opinions and speculations. How can I teach you about Zen unless you first empty your cup?"

Our minds and hearts are just like this cup—*we need to empty ourselves and unlearn what we are*, in order to become who we want to be.

Life, sometimes, isn't about becoming, as much as it is about unbecoming everything that we are. Our spiritual journey is not so much about becoming something, as it is about unbecoming everything—that we added on since birth—to go back to being the pure, innocent, loving beings that we are. This entails shedding all the layers of our ego, to drop our strong points of view, our opinions, our complaints, our demands, our biases, our negativity, our anger, our need for control, our grievances. We have to identify all the layers that we have to shed.

So many of us are living our lives as if the beliefs, thoughts and stories we hold about ourselves are the unshakeable truth. We become so deeply involved with what we have learnt about ourselves, our culture and this world; and what others want and expect from us, that we have forgotten who we truly are. We have forgotten who we are beneath the masks that we wear. This realization can be both illuminating and grief-inducing at the same time.

The first step to *Becoming Whole* is to acknowledge that you have imbibed certain response mechanisms, which continue to cause conflict and drama in your life, which need to be unlearned. The more you resist acknowledging that you have incorporated these traits, the more these traits become ingrained in you. That which you resist, persists. Acknowledging and accepting that you need to unlearn first, in order to relearn, is the hardest part to do and, yet, the most vital step in your journey to self-heal.

Keep un-layering. Keep unraveling. Keep inquiring. Keep digging. Keep questioning. Keep seeking. And then, practice accepting what you find.

It is enough that you are on the path. The path will unfold. It will reveal itself to you in its perfect timing, and all is really well.

Inside-Outside

The outside is always a reflection of the inside.
Very small shifts inside can lead to major miracles on the outside.
Once you figure this out, by trial and error, you begin to understand how this Universe works.
Vibration is the key.
Tune the inside so it is in harmony with the vibration of the Universe.
Instinct is better than intellect; gut is stronger than brain; heart is all.
Deep inside your own being, you will discover the magical portal.
Step through—and you disappear!
Only magic remains—inside and outside and everywhere.
It's so simple that it seems complex.

You become the eye of the storm, the still center of the hurricane.
All you do is stay there.
Life will go on with greater intensity: but the center will remain motionless, still, silent.
The only way to check it out is to play with your own inner tuning.
Harmony is Being and Consciousness and Bliss.
Become it—and you will find it everywhere.
And miracles will effortlessly appear.
This is how it is.

PART 1

DEEP HEALING

I

THE UNIVERSE RESPONDS TO YOUR VIBRATION

---

*Think of the Universe as a place that **wants** to give you everything.*

The Universe wants to give you all the abundance, all the well-being, all the love, all the support that you need and desire. All you need to do is put yourself in a frequency of receiving all that you are asking for. Just like you must tune into the radio station you want to listen to, you have to be tuned into the energy you want to manifest in your life.

So, what is 'the Universe'? *The Universe* is simply everything that exists, it is basically made up of energy. Being spiritual is being able to harness, connect and embrace this energy. The Source. Divine Energy. Consciousness. The Universe. Each of these names, perfect in their own way, are used interchangeably to describe this body of universal energy.

What is Consciousness? Consciousness is the higher power, the all-pervading, all-powerful Divine Energy that runs this Universe. Consciousness is made of you and you are made of Consciousness.

You are an extension of Source or Consciousness and an enormously powerful co-creator in this Universe and hence, an integral part of it. Whether you use words or thoughts to express your desires, your frequency is matched, *every single time*. In the realm of all possibilities, everything you want already exists. You just have to breathe life into those possibilities with your vibrations.

You are Consciousness. You are Energy. You are Vibration.

Chapter by chapter, this book will help you to make a shift in the frequency that you emanate through your thoughts and feelings. As you become whole, one layer at a time, you will start vibrating at a higher frequency—at the frequency of your desires—and it is only a matter of time before you see them manifest in the physical realm in your life.

Think of the Universe as a place that wants to give you everything, and whatever you are not getting is because you are unable to receive it.

The Universe responds to the frequency of your thoughts and words. Your thoughts run at many levels, and, whether you realize it or not, every situation in your life you have attracted to yourself— even the unexpected and undesirable ones. You might not be consciously aware of this, but you attract your own circumstances because of some belief or attitude that you hold in your mind. Your deep-rooted beliefs and thoughts about your own worthiness and deservedness shapes your life in the physical realm.

You are not being punished or rewarded; you are only being matched.

For example, you have probably been taking the time for your personal and spiritual growth, to explore your emotions, and become more in tune with yourself. That's how you attracted even this book into your life—to help you to experience a deeper understanding of yourself—it is no coincidence.

As the founder of a holistic wellness company called *Begin to Heal*, which connects you to a large group of coaches, healers and holistic doctors in the US, I was invited to speak frequently on panels, radio shows and podcasts in New York. During such engagements, I spoke actively about the role our thoughts play in attracting the circumstances in our life—both the desirable and the undesirable ones—and as expected, this uncomfortable truth was not received well by everyone. It is difficult to acknowledge and accept, even to ourselves, that we are the cause of our suffering, but the truth is that we are.

Before I started to speak about this simple, yet profound law of the Universe, I took years to truly understand and internalize it myself. I realized that I was attracting stressful situations and experiences into my life through my thoughts and feelings, which led to my adrenal fatigue health issue. It was in my control to change the frequency I was emitting with my own subconscious thoughts to attract all the well-being in the universe! I had to unlearn old ways of thinking, feeling, and expressing myself and relearn new habits and beliefs, which helped me to change my vibration and to start attracting all that my heart desired.

Perhaps you have tried the Law of Attraction before and wondered why it doesn't seem to work for you. You've read 'The Secret', you share positive quotes, you say and do all the right things, and it *still* doesn't seem to work. And you're left wondering, "Why not?"

This is because you are missing out on the most important ingredient—*believing, truly believing, at your core that you deserve to receive that blessing, that you are worthy of it.* Do you, at some level, consciously or subconsciously believe that you don't deserve all the blessings? That you are not good enough for them or some other self-limiting thought? When you believe such thoughts, the universe will respond to *that* deep-rooted belief, *not* to the superficial efforts you are making.

Whatever is your dominant thought, feeling or belief, will become your vibration.

Know this—every positive or negative experience in your life is a direct result of a belief held inside your mind. Yes, even that boss who takes credit for your work, your partner who controls you, and that friend who betrays you—*all* of it has been attracted by you in your life.

Which means that you need to take complete accountability for everything that goes on in your life, instead of shifting blame outside of yourself. A vibrational Universe does not punish or reward you, there are no victims from its perspective, it only matches your vibration.

How do you know if you are emitting the right frequency to receive? Through your feelings. Your feelings will tell you how authentically you are aligned with your desires. Feel good when you think about your wants, even when you don't have them, and that's how you practice changing your vibration. If you are feeling good about receiving that blessing, then you are emitting the right energy to attract it into your life. Your frequency will match your most consistent thoughts and feelings, which basically become your belief system.

Your life is simply the manifestation of your own consciousness, through the energy that you emanate.

If you feel that the world is unfair to you and friends cannot be trusted, you will attract situations where your friends break your trust. If you believe that all men/women cheat, you will attract men/women that will cheat on you. The angry attract the angry, the cheerful attract other cheerful people, intense people will attract other intense people. Like attracts like, this is the law. A person who has anger inside them, will attract other angry people, as it activates the same latent anger inside the other person.

Your own sense of who you are and what you deserve, attracts the kind of experiences that will make you feel more of that about you.

For example, if you are needy and insecure, life will send you emotionally unavailable people to match your frequency of neediness, in turn making you feel even more needy. The Universe will also put you in conversations where other people will mirror back to you what you feel about yourself. You attract rejection because there is a part of you that wants to feel this rejection, you attract suffering because at some deep subconscious level, you enjoy the drama, the self-pity and the attention you receive from others. You will not experience an undesirable situation unless there is a part of you that wants to feel that way.

If you are feeling guilt or shame about something, you will suddenly find yourself in a conversation where someone evokes more of *that* guilt in you. If you feel you are not that smart, you will attract comments from friends who make fun of you for not being that smart. You attract such conversations and feedback from others because the universe is reflecting the messages *you have for yourself*, through these people. It is not what they are thinking of you, it is what you are thinking of yourself. These people are only mirroring or reflecting your own thoughts back to you.

What you feel you deserve to receive in life, is exactly what you will receive. Make no mistake, *you* are in your own way. Nothing—or no one—else is.

The energy of your vibrational signal is determined by what you think about and how you feel. And others respond to your signal accordingly. If you are vibrating at the frequency of love, joy and abundance, you are going to attract things to support that frequency. If you are vibrating at the frequency of disappointment, you are going to attract things of a similar vibration to support that frequency.

Why would the Universe do that to us? Because the only way to get you to change that belief or attitude which is holding you back in life, is by putting you in situations where you are forced to meet your demons and transcend that self-limiting belief you hold deep in your subconscious mind. Once you change that sub-conscious thought and start feeling better about yourself and deserving of more, you will attract the objects of your heart's desires to you. So, when you stop being needy and insecure, situations and people that perpetuate that feeling and make you feel needy or insecure will disappear.

If you are suffering, ask yourself, *what about suffering do I enjoy?* If you are surrounded by drama and conflict, ask yourself, *what about drama and conflict do I like?* Did you grow up in a house where conflict or drama was the norm and the way to build connections with one another? Or, perhaps, it gives you an opportunity to attract attention and sympathy to yourself?

You cannot continue to believe in what you have and expect to change what you attract. You have to understand that what you think, what you believe, what you feel, and what you attract are all correlated. Become happy with who you are, with what you have, and then ask for more from that place of gratitude and contentment, and the vibrational universe will respond with more. It is all about your mindset, from the moment you wake up to when you sleep. Everything is up to you. Your emotions, your thoughts, your perceptions, your reactions. Freedom from unwanted experiences can never be achieved by trying to control the behavior of others. It can only be achieved by changing and raising your own vibration to attract the experiences you want.

You are a Vibrational Being in a Vibrational Universe. When you are in Vibrational Harmony with the frequency of your desires, everything you want flows to you with ease.

So, how can you change your vibration and change what you attract in your life?

When *you* feel worthy and deserving of all that your heart desires, you will become a magnet for all the well-being in the universe. The purpose of this book is to bring you in alignment with yourself, one with your divinity. When you're aligned, you stay centered within you and less moved by the things outside of you.

The minute you decide you want better for yourself, is the minute the entire universe shifts in your favor. Your declaration, your intentions, your changed actions and prayers begin the creation of a new reality for you.

>*A belief is only a practised vibration.* —Abraham Hicks

The good news is that this vibrational universe empowers you, so, if you don't like your life the way it is, you can change how you think and feel about it, and the Universe will respond accordingly. The way to consciously stop thinking one thought is by activating another, by *deliberately taking your attention away from a self-limiting belief to an empowering one to change your frequency* to a higher state of being, and go from feeling insecure to secure, from feeling unwanted to feeling loved. Seeing ourselves as responsible for the energy we bring to a situation means we are always connected with our ability to change, control or transform our inner and outer realities.

Language is another way to align with the power of the Universe so that it can work on your behalf. *Your words have power*, what you say repeatedly becomes your vibration and that is exactly what will happen for you. So, be very mindful of what you say, the Universe is always listening. Positive words help to retune your frequency, and slowly, you will start vibrating at a higher level.

Consciousness is always broadcasting frequencies of love, clarity, connection, wholeness, and expansion. All we need to do is become a vibrational match to these frequencies. If you have the ability to imagine it, the Universe has the ability—and the resources—to deliver it unto you. In full.

What if you start believing that everything you desire is already making its way to you and you never had any reason to stress to begin with? See yourself receiving a powerful light from Source, giving you everything you want through this stream of light. Imagine yourself receiving all the abundance you need, feel worthy of receiving it. Ask that anything that doesn't allow you to be in full vibrational alignment with the Universe, is uncreated from your mind right now. The degree to which you receive it shows your ability to receive, and to the extent you don't receive it, shows your degree of resistance.

As Abraham Hick says,

"You are not days, weeks, months away from your heart's desires, you are only a vibration away."

This Law of Vibration grants your every wish, your every desire, your every prayer. Just allow things to flow into your life. The art of receiving, allowing things to come in, is a practised vibration and once you learn it, you become part of the creative energy of the universe. There is no shortage, no lack, only the allowing or disallowing of what one is asking for.

Affirmations to raise your Vibration:

Repeat 3 times

In the infinity of life where I am,

All is perfect, whole and complete

I live in harmony and balance with everyone I know

Deep at the center of my being, there is an infinite well of love

I now allow this love to flow to the surface

And fill my heart, my mind, my body, my consciousness

And radiate out from me in all directions

And return to me multiplied.

The Seed

The seed of intention planted in the mind inevitably bears fruit of its own accord.

Conscious, positive intention produces positive results.

Unconscious, negative intention produces negative results.

It's as simple as that. So be sure you chose the right seed.

The seed born of intuition grows into a powerful, unstoppable force.

It commands the power that forms the universe and attracts all it needs for growth, without effort and without fail.

Infinite energy works unceasingly and automatically to deliver perfection.

This is the everyday magic that keeps all creation going.

Be aware of the empty sky that is the background of thoughts and emotions—they appear, change shape, float and disappear like the clouds;

The sky remains untouched, unchanged.

You are not the clouds; you are the sky.

Here, you will discover that total emptiness is absolute fullness.

Here, in this infinitely fertile sky of creation, plant your seed.

Perfection blossoms like a lotus flower.

EVERYONE
IS YOUR MIRROR

*We come to understand ourselves best through
our relationships with other people.*

We attract individuals into our lives who mirror who we are. Those we feel drawn to, reflect our inner self back to us, and we also act as a mirror for them.

Simply put, when you look at others, you will likely see what exists in you. When you see qualities which you admire in others like courage, innocence, patience, or any light in the soul of another, you are seeing the goodness that resides within your own soul. When you see traits in others that evoke feelings of anger, annoyance, or hatred in you, you are seeing those parts of yourself that you have disowned or disliked, reflected back at you through these people.

Let's elaborate a bit on this concept, also known as Projection.

When we do not acknowledge our own unpleasant thoughts, motivations, desires, or feelings, we ascribe those characteristics to others. Such blaming and fault-finding is called Projection. Through projection, it becomes easier for us to accuse others of

doing what, in fact, we are doing.

Projection **is our unconscious way of denying the existence**
of something inside ourselves and attributing it to
others and externalizing it.

Every single person, and the way you perceive them, is a projection
of your own thoughts, stories, beliefs, and prejudices. We throw all
the uncomfortable feelings and shame we feel for ourselves, onto
others, because we don't want to deal with this shame ourselves. *We*
land up making others feel guilty for who we are, because we shy away
from wanting to feel that guilt ourselves.

Our worlds are a projection of our inner state. What you think about
others isn't about *them*, it's about *you.*

It is easy to see the traits you do not like in others. It is way more
difficult to realize that you possess those same traits. For instance,
a truly innocent and straightforward person cannot recognize
manipulation in another, unless they are manipulative too. A
calm person cannot recognize aggression in another unless they
have it too. You simply cannot recognize a trait in another unless
your own soul is familiar with it too. When we take ownership of
our undesirable traits, we are less likely to project our disowned
qualities onto others.

So, when you see something that you intensely dislike in another,
you can be sure that trait exists in you as well.

Who you are, can be laid bare to you through what you see in others! The attitudes, behaviors and traits of others are linked to our unconscious and unresolved issues. We can only be triggered strongly by something when we experience our own traits in others. The trait we dislike most about any other person, is the same trait we dislike most in ourselves. We, then, tend to judge and criticize others, but we are truly judging and criticizing ourselves without even realizing it.

Because we are all mirrors for each other, looking around at the people in your life will tell you a lot about yourself. Your biggest opportunity to grow will come from your closest relationships, like your parents, your siblings, your closest friends, your partner. When you see any of them as flawed, you are actually seeing your own flaws in them. There is no exception to this law.

What you see in others exists in you.

Everyone is Your Teacher

We all have an inner compass that attracts us to certain people and makes us shy away from others. Emotions form our internal GPS as we progress through life, seeking bliss and enlightenment, and every person we meet evokes guiding emotions within us. We're just like magnets, constantly attracting or repelling each other. The force is the same—no matter its direction. Its value too is the same, hence, attraction is the same as repulsion. They teach us the same thing, but from opposite perspectives.

People you like show you what you wish to be, while people you don't like, show you what you don't wish to be.

The value of those different categories of individuals is the same, just like joy and pain are equally valuable to your personal development. When you understand this, it no longer makes sense to dislike the people you currently dislike. Instead, be grateful for every single person you meet, no matter what emotional effect they have on you. They are all here to teach you something about you. Since our purpose in life is to discover what we don't love, and learn to love it, the people who get on our nerves the most are among our greatest teachers!

The people outside of you are only revealing your conscious and subconscious patterns back to you.

Let me share an anecdote from my life.

I used to get triggered whenever someone would tell me what to do or not to do, or if I was micromanaged in any way. Since I have been independent from a young age, I don't enjoy being controlled or to live my life according to other people's expectations of me. I realized that I get triggered by that because that's exactly what I was doing to others, telling everyone else how to live their life and what changes they need to incorporate in their behavior or life to become a better person. I realized I would treat people like projects, always focusing on what needed to change in them. It also made me realize that I didn't truly accept people the way that they are, and I was attracting the same non-acceptance, criticism, and control into my life from my loved ones. Life was mirroring my own behavior back to me. If I don't like to be told what to do, then why would others like to hear that from me? These people who were triggering me were actually my biggest mirrors showing me what I needed to learn about myself.

**Be eternally grateful to everyone who triggers you,
for they are your biggest teachers.**

I invite you to make a note every time you get triggered negatively by certain characteristics in someone's personality for the next two to three weeks. You will find, if you look into it deep and long enough, it represents issues from your past that have gone unresolved. An example of this would be attracting people who betray you because you have not dealt with an abandonment issue from your past. What you are seeing reflected back to you from life is your own belief that you cannot trust anyone. Or, let's say, you have a constant need to prove to others that you are 'right'. Chances are, you will attract people who strongly disagree with you because they also have the need to convince others to agree with them. If you resent controlling and judgmental people, invariably you will have controlling and judgmental tendencies within you. Maybe you believe that your partner is self-centered? You are only going to heal when you realize that there is a part of you which is self-centered too.

Everyone around you serves as a mirror.

If you find yourself nodding your head just now, or introspecting or reflecting, congratulations! You've just expanded your self-awareness. Here's what you can do. From now on, when you find yourself triggered by a person or situation, ask yourself:

"What is this person showing me about me that I need to learn?"

"Do I behave like this now, or did I behave like this before?"

Craving or demanding that the other person change, reflects our own pain. Embrace where they are now and encourage their growth by demonstrating change in yourself first. Every person we meet in life is showing up at the right time in our lives to show us what we need to heal within ourselves. The people with whom you interact are showing you who you are, and ultimately, providing you with an opportunity to love and accept yourself. When you love and accept yourself for that trait inside you, you will love and accept the other person automatically too. *It all begins with you.*

> ***Be grateful for whoever comes, because each has been sent as a guide from beyond.*** **—Rumi**

Why are you Attracting Rejection?

Do you often feel rejected by others? By a partner, your colleagues, your parents, or your friends? We now know that it is our vibration, our frequency, that attracts all desirable and undesirable experiences into our lives. The way we treat others is a reflection of the relationship we have with ourselves. If we like ourselves, we will like others too. If we judge ourselves, we will judge others too. If you self-reject, others will reject you too.

The fact that you are facing rejection in life may indicate one of two things—you may either be judging and rejecting yourself first; or, you might be rejecting others before they are rejecting you. *Even though you have a pleasant, friendly demeanour, what others pick up*

*is the energy of your self-rejection and self-judgment and they end up
rejecting you too.* When you are rejected, the person is reflecting
back to you what you believe to be true about yourself—that
subconscious belief that something is wrong with you. Do you
think you aren't good enough? Then bam! Someone will come
along to prove you right. The Universe just matched your vibration!

As human beings, we oscillate between self-serving distortions
and harsh self-criticism. So, while we want to show the world how
amazing we are, beneath the surface, our inner critic is emitting
frequencies of self-rejection, and hence, attracting rejection from
others as well. When we choose and chase partners or friends who
don't respond back to us in equal measure, we are telling them how
to treat us. We are rejecting ourselves before they reject us. The
more they withdraw, the more our longing to have them in our life
increases. For instance, you might insist on becoming friends with
someone at work who says yes to your coffee invites, but bails at the
last minute every time. But, instead of writing the person off, you
try to win them over. When we feel rejected, we often turn against
ourselves, and begin to believe that the only person who can make us
feel okay again is the very person who has rejected us. And therein
begins our endless chase for their attention and approval.

**_Our chronic need for chasing unavailable relationships is an act of
self-rejection too._**

The other likelihood is that you are subconsciously rejecting these
people before they reject you. Chances are, you may not even
realize that reality. At a subconscious level, you don't truly like this
person. Everything is energetic, even if you don't tell them directly

that you don't like them, you emit a vibe of judgment or rejection toward them. This is picked up by their subconscious. They can sense that you don't like them, and they reject you before you can reject them, in an attempt to protect themselves.

I know I have been in situations when some friends suddenly disconnected from me. They stopped responding to my texts or calls or they seemed to be avoiding me. And I had no idea why. I realized that in each of those situations I had been judging or rejecting them in my mind. And even though I never told them that's what I was thinking, my thoughts were telepathically or energetically transferred to them. I might have been thinking about walking out of their life, they just beat me to it and that hurt my pride. *Fact is, that I had rejected them in my subconscious, way before they rejected me in my conscious life!*

Our energy, our vibe, our body language, our comments— everything emits a frequency which can be, and is, picked up by others.

You will stop inviting rejection from others into your life when you stop rejecting yourself, and when you stop rejecting others. When you like yourself, you are in harmony with your self-worth and with the Universe or Source within you. When that is the case, your appreciation of others flows abundantly too.

Here's something I find useful to remember:

All rejection is redirection.

Sometimes when something doesn't work out, be grateful for it—

you don't know what you're being protected from or where you're being guided to next. Everything that happens to you, is happening *for you*. Trust that what the universe is removing from your life is for your greatest good.

So, when it seems like things are going against you and life seems so unfair in *this moment*, it might just be an amazing stroke of luck in the long run. Haven't you witnessed this many times in your life, when you look back in life, and have been so grateful that things didn't work out the way you had hoped, back then, they would? This is the Universe's way of protecting you and bringing you in alignment with what is best for your highest self. Trust in Divine Timing. Even if it's hard to see the bigger picture in the moment, believe that everything you are experiencing right now is for your highest good. Allow time and space for everything to unfold exactly how and when it should.

Maybe, *just maybe*, the things that are the hardest are actually the greatest. Because they have the potential to wake you up. Because they can give you the clarity you never knew you needed to see all of the things your soul has been longing for you to see. So that you could finally evolve and become the person you were destined to be. The struggle, the surrender, the patience, the growing pains, the stress, the calm—all have a purpose.

Be ok with not knowing what will come next, but know whatever it is, you will be okay.

Stress is just a perception reinforced by our conditioning. Next time something stresses you out, ask yourself, "*How would I be, if*

I didn't apply meaning to this? How would it be if I treated this as just another passing moment like any other?" So, instead of getting stressed when faced with rejection, just don't apply any meaning to it and know that all rejection is just redirection.

Your Life Reflects Your Inner State

The relationship you have with yourself determines the relationship you will have with others. If you hold yourself to high standards, you hold others to those standards too. If you love yourself, you will love others too. If you are peaceful inside, you will have peace in your life too. If your mind is a battlefield, and internally you are constantly at war with what is available externally—complaining, whining, blaming—or you are at war with yourself, then that will be mirrored outside of you as well. If you are calm inside and at peace when you are alone and you are generating thoughts of peace and love, then that will be reflected in your life.

Your life is always a mirror of what's going on inside you.

When you fix what is inside first, the outside will fall into place automatically. Most people have this backward, they think their circumstances define their inner happiness when it is the opposite that is actually true.

Byron Katie, the author, teaches us how to change our stories about others by turning around our thoughts or opinion of them, into a thought or opinion we actually hold of ourselves. This helps us learn to see our own projections—thereby giving us the inner freedom that we need by releasing such thoughts. For example,

If you feel that "Pooja dislikes me", then you could turn around that thought in two ways. You could either say "I dislike Pooja" or "I dislike myself".

Let that sink in.

You will realize that at least one, if not both turnarounds will resonate with you. If we have a strong dislike for someone, it is common for us to protect ourselves by projecting our feelings of dislike onto that person

-   If you feel that "My partner is abandoning me", try turning that around by saying, "*I* am abandoning my partner" OR "*I* am abandoning myself" and see if either or both of those turnarounds feel true. Repeat the turnarounds a few times to yourself and you will realize that *that's where the truth lies.* You were only projecting your own feelings onto your partner.

-   If you feel that your boss is a control freak, try turning that around to "I am controlling"—it will undoubtedly resonate with you.

We are always projecting our thoughts and feelings onto other people. Even if the other person does feel that way about you, *the only part you have control on is how you feel about them.*

The less judgments and conditions you impose on yourself to deserve your own love and acceptance, the easier it becomes to love and accept others as they are too. The first step is to accept that these traits exist in you, then, instead of judging yourself for having them, be compassionate toward yourself and start the process of unlearning that behavior. Slowly, you will begin to accept these traits in the other person too; or, in the very least, you will start seeing these people from a compassionate lens. So, heal your thoughts first, become aware of your projections, that's half the battle won already! When you can first accept that trait in *you*, you will accept it in others, too, with a lot more compassion.

We can only love and accept others to the degree that we love and accept ourselves. If you don't love and accept yourself fully, how can others love and accept you?

Once you become aware of your unwanted traits, you can start releasing them. When you lose former versions of yourself, like shedding old skin, it may feel strange at first. A lot of negative emotions like anger, sorrow, etc. may come up. Know that it is ok to grieve the versions of yourself you are letting go of, so that you can step more into your own light. When you start believing in yourself, living in your worth, you will feel like grieving your past when you spent a lot of time doing the opposite. Honor this grief, as it reminds you of your growth. As time passes, and you get comfortable in honoring yourself as a new way of being, you will feel a huge surge of relief, followed by love for yourself. One of the hardest, yet most magical, things you will ever do is to learn to love yourself. That's how pain and fear subside—when love becomes our dominant vibration. This is how we become who we truly are meant to be— loving, peaceful souls, at ease with ourselves, as well as with others.

Affirmations:

Repeat 3 Times

I am grateful for all that I am, have, give, and receive.

I let go of any judgments of myself, easily and effortlessly.

I let go of any judgments of others, easily and effortlessly.

I love and accept myself fully, completely, and unconditionally.

I love and accept everyone, completely, and unconditionally.

I treat everyone with unconditional acceptance, dignity, and love.

I approach any triggering situation in my life with love, kindness, and respect.

I inspire others to live a life of wholeness, harmony, and meaning.

The Mirror Mind

When the attention dives inward, mind-chatter sinks and dissolves in the Heart.
This results in stillness.
Stillness is the Heart, the eternal, ever-present beginning, the place of rest, renewal and re-birth, the infinite silence that is the Self.
When the attention re-surfaces from the depths of being, the clouds of thought and feeling vanish before the rising sun of Self.
Empty blue sky expands into infinity.
The clear mirror reflects the original truth.
The sweet scent of peace fills the void.
Outer and Inner become one.
Everything is radiant with magic once again.
This Heart is your true home, your very nature.
Stay here—and all will be well.

III

WHAT ARE YOUR TRIGGERS REVEALING TO YOU?

Does this happen to you? You get this feeling when someone makes a jokingly mean comment that might not be a huge deal to that person, but it totally destabilizes you for the rest of the day? Suddenly, you find yourself feeling off-center and thrust into bouts of anger, anxiety, guilt, fear, or shame. You might even lose control and hurt them back with your words, volume, expressions or actions.

Sound familiar? You have just been triggered.

Emotional triggers are people, words, opinions, situations, or environmental situations that provoke an intense emotional reaction within us. Some common emotional triggers could be someone rejecting you, leaving you, discounting or ignoring you, controlling you, giving you a disapproving look, or someone being judgmental or critical of you. Emotional triggers are stored in your subconscious mind and are activated again and again. The stronger the emotional response you have to situations, the more easily you can be triggered when similar situations reoccur.

Be grateful to this emotion for what it can teach you.

These triggers are bringing up parts of you that need to be acknowledged or healed. So, honor these triggers as a way of becoming whole, not a block to becoming. If you find yourself triggered, it means that you are ready to heal one of these two parts in you:

a) Unhealed wounds or unmet needs

-   *Unhealed wounds*, usually from childhood, are incidents from your childhood that may not have been addressed, or unmet needs that now continue to manifest as patterns in your adult life. This is the biggest reason behind most of the triggers in your life. Being emotionally triggered always goes back to some unmet need of acceptance, attention, love, safety, respect, being needed, or being valued. Identifying that unhealed wound and the unmet need behind that wound, which is the real source of your pain, is a big part of healing yourself. Inner Child Healing Therapy (which has gained momentum globally amongst therapists and healers alike as a highly effective therapy to heal all kinds of triggers, depression, stress and anxiety) can help you to go back to your childhood to resolve these unmet needs and past wounds.

b) Ego preservation

-   *Ego preservation* is another big reason for feeling defensive against these triggers. This artificial identity of "I" that we hold onto is composed of thoughts, memories, cultural values, assumptions, and belief structures that we have developed in order to fit into society. We all have an ego and its primary purpose is to feel self-righteous or have the illusion of control. When we are challenged or hurt by others, we are prone to becoming triggered—immediately. We will argue, insult, belittle, defame, backstab, sabotage, and assault people who pose a threat to our ego's survival. This pain is inevitable as long as you identify yourself as your mind and your ego, and as long as you keep playing the ego's game of one-upmanship.

Beneath every behavior is a feeling, and beneath every feeling there is a need. When we meet that need, rather than focus on that behavior, we begin to deal with the cause and not the symptom.

You must have also noticed that life sends you the same problem again and again through different people, partners, different friends, different situations. You will keep attracting the same situation again and again until you have learnt the lesson that situation is trying to teach you, until you transcend that behavior, that attitude, that fear inside you which attracted that trigger in the first place.

Every time you are tempted to react in the same old way, ask yourself, "Do I want to remain a prisoner of my past? Or do I want to show up in a more conscious way in this present moment?"

And remember, if it wasn't this person in this situation, it would be someone, or something else showing up to trigger the same thing in you—until you heal the pattern that attracted this in the first place. To face these challenges means you need to first accept the fact that there is something *within* you which keeps attracting the same type of person or the same type of situation, as painful as that awareness might be.

Triggers occur with the intention of self-discovery and to encourage you to heal and release unresolved energies that are ready to be brought into wholeness to set you free.

With practice, you will see that people who trigger you the most, have qualities and behaviors of people you had the most conflicted relationships with, in the past. We project the conflicted-parent relationship on to others the most. We should be grateful to these triggers for showing us what needs to be healed, and what emotions are lying dormant. If you are looking to evolve, then every next level of life will demand a different version of you, and a more evolved response to these situations.

When you get triggered next, ask yourself what this situation is revealing to you about yourself, take a moment to pause, curb the desire to counterattack or excuse yourself from the situation. Take the time to calm down and just don't react at all. *Not giving someone who is trying to provoke you, a reaction when they desperately seek it, is very powerful.* When you stop getting provoked or triggered by someone, people realize that their words are having no impact on you anymore and they stop provoking you going forward.

Reclaiming your power is the process of realizing that no person, no situation can take away your ability to choose how you behave, you are always the one governing your actions.

Learning to go inwards during a trigger allows you to respond rather than react, to heal your wounds and have a better relationship with your unmet needs or wounds. For most of us, it boils down to two things—a desire to be seen and a desire to be heard. On the surface, it can manifest as jealousy, insecurity, anger, rejection, control. Deep inside, however, each one of these emotions stems from a place of insecurity, which in turn stems from a very basic human need to be *seen or heard*. To be acknowledged, to be noticed, to be understood.

Learning to master this chaos in you, *will* help you to balance your emotions. An emotion only controls our thinking when we are not present. When we are present, aware, and watching our emotions, our narratives cannot feed it through unconscious identification. It is challenging to create change in ourselves if we keep digging our heels deeper into our old identities by repeating old patterns of behaviors. Being present in this moment is enough to dissolve the past and bring attention to what is happening within, without analyzing it or judging it.

To be able to show up in the same places with the same people, facing the same triggers, and to respond differently, now that is the growth you are looking for.

What is the way to this growth? While there are multiple ways to get there—many modalities, many ways, many teachers—at the end of the day, it is still *you* who needs to do the work, and *you* that needs to heal.

Inner Child Healing

Each and every one of us holds on to unhealed wounds from our childhood, regardless of how loving our upbringing was. A part of us grows up and one other part stays a child. The part that grows up, may not always have got what it needed as a child. Our inability to process what was said to us or what happened to or with us as a child, can cause us to respond defensively or negatively to that trigger for the rest of our lives.

Reparenting our inner child means giving to ourselves what we needed as children and might not have received from our parents. We realize that our parents did the best they could, yet, we need to heal our scars. Inner Child Healing work invites you to do exactly that and release any residual blame or anger toward them.

We develop a survival response mechanism and sometimes, we can become like a fortress especially in cases of severe childhood trauma. We put up a shield, in the form of a behavioral pattern, so that our pain never gets exposed and we don't get hurt again. So, we need to find new ways to adapt and respond to such triggers that bring up these emotional wounds from our childhood.

Having said that, not all wounds are big negative experiences in childhood. Sometimes they are normal aspects of growing up, which we allow to affect us through our adult lives, without even realizing it. For example, when a younger sibling is born in the family, the older sibling begins to feel neglected and unloved, and they play out this wound their whole life. It is imperative to heal our inner child to stop playing out our wounds in repeated cycles. The best way to facilitate your own healing is to consciously parent the child-self that is present within you and honor your own unmet needs.

We will always be emotionally needy if we wait for someone else to lovingly parent the underdeveloped parts of ourselves. We will always be powerless if we wait for someone else to rescue the part of us that needs to be rescued. And we will always be unhealed if we wait for someone else to take care of the part of us that needs to be cared for.

You need to provide for yourself today what you haven't received in the past from others.

Love your inner child and become your own nurturing parent, so that even if you lose other relationships, you can trust that you are whole, safe, and complete.

What if each of these triggers is preparing you to become the person you should be? When we are triggered, we get carried away by the hurt or pain that this trigger evoked. Our natural response, then, is to counterattack and shift blame, or become defensive and attack. All counterattack is self-destructive behavior. The worst part about such self-destructive behavior is that it can be a bit addictive; and leaving it behind feels like killing that part of you which taught you how to survive.

All attack and counterattack is the transference of guilt, you will never attack anyone in your life, unless you have guilt.

The best way to deal with this—and this is a process that requires time and discipline—is to train your mind to be stronger than the pull of your emotions. Till the time you are able to master this, you will lose yourself, every single time. You will continue to suffer if you have an emotional reaction to everything that is said to you. If words control you, then everything can control you.

True power is in restraint. Allow things to pass. When we don't take things personally, we have more room to forgive and free ourselves of the past.

Healing Our Triggers

So how can we heal our triggers?

Let your spiritual expansion begin with emotional authenticity. Nothing to hide, nowhere to run. Once you identify the unmet need or the negative belief held by you, substitute that thought with a more positive and forgiving one. By doing this, you might still get annoyed when that trigger shows up again, but it will not take over your mental-emotional energies; and will allow you to respond with more grace to that provocation. *Learning to respond with grace even when others don't, is a practiced art, and a giant step in your evolution.* This will allow you to start observing yourself instead of reacting emotionally in different situations and allow you to choose your response. Once you stop getting provoked by that trigger, that situation or that trigger will automatically stop showing up.

If you ignore evolving, the situation will keep coming back in repeated cycles in your life. The lesson repeats until we have healed it or brought it into conscious completion. It repeats until we no longer react and take back our power to consciously respond and elevate higher. It repeats until we acknowledge that we deserve better than what no longer serves us. We are the only ones who can rewrite our destiny. No one else holds that power but us. Once the lesson is learnt, the situation will stop repeating itself.

So, Evolve or Repeat. Those are your only choices.

Some other ways to heal yourself of the impact of these triggers could be to go to a professional therapist or a spiritual coach to heal your triggers or you can try one of these healing techniques.

a) *Healing Your Inner Child*- Take 3 deep breaths, breathing in from your nose and breathing out through your mouth and close your eyes. Hold compassion for yourself and go back to those moments from your past or your childhood when you didn't feel seen or heard. Now imagine yourself (at your current age), talking to that younger version of yourself—in that moment of your childhood when you were a child or a teenager when the wound occurred for the first time—and tell that child, "I see you", "I hear you", "You are enough", "I will protect you", "I love you". Do this often, and slowly your inner child will begin to heal.

b) *Journaling*- Start to journal every time you are triggered, how that made you feel, and why you think you reacted the way you did. You will learn so much about yourself this way, as you read your own reactions. Writing is a powerful way to bring things out and create a record of your patterns. Each time this is practiced you become more and more aware of your thoughts and actions.

Observe a trigger and your pent up emotions related to it. Identify a journal. In this, write down all thoughts and feelings associated with that trigger as you experienced it today, and in the past. Write down all your thoughts about the person, the thought, the situation, the relationship, the word, the expression that triggered you, what that makes you feel about it/them, how that makes you feel, write it all down. There are no right or wrong thoughts, write them all down. If you choose to not write these in a journal, you can even write everything down on a piece of paper. Then when you are done, burn that paper. This simple technique can be highly relief inducing.

c) *EFT Tapping*- Release all past wounds through EFT tapping. Emotional Freedom Technique (EFT) Tapping is a type of alternative psychological acupressure therapy which involves tapping fingers on specific points on your head and face in a particular sequence, to clear negative emotions. It is an amazingly simple, powerful and effective technique that can be used to clear any trigger, stress, anxiety, depression or anger, or any other deeply held beliefs. As you keep tapping these 8 points in sequence, say clearing statements to express how you are feeling, how sad, how angry, how unloved, how disrespected you are feeling, whatever it is that you are feeling and release those pent up emotions. EFT is a widely used technique amongst coaches and therapists to heal their clients, there are large EFT conferences that are held every year to discover the benefits of this powerful tool.

d) *Cleansing Prayer*- Try saying this prayer three times. You can repeat these as you tap your EFT points, or you can say them without tapping as well, the choice is yours.

"I am now choosing to cleanse myself.

I release all thoughts and feelings of sadness, loneliness, fear, anger, suspicion, and resentment, that are no longer of service to my highest and greatest good, across lifetimes, space, and dimensions.

I pray that all such energies be transmuted to love for my highest good, and so it is."

e) ***Metta or Loving Kindness Meditation-*** If you have a persistently difficult relationship with a particular person in your life who manages to trigger you a lot, then you can heal the dynamic with this person by doing the Metta Loving Kindness Meditation for 21 days. Research shows that it takes 21 days to rewire any subconscious patterns or habits or feelings about someone, so if you do anything consistently for 21 days, it can change your internal "wiring". Loving-kindness meditation consists primarily of our intention of wishing ourselves or others happiness and love. By doing this meditation for 5 minutes a day, you can take off the negative charge in your dynamic with this person and deal with any ongoing problem from a place of kindness.

To practice this loving-kindness meditation, sit in a comfortable and relaxed manner. Take two or three deep breaths with slow, long and complete exhalations. Metta is first practiced toward oneself since we can only love others when we love ourselves first. Sitting quietly, mentally repeat—slowly, and steadily—the following phrases for yourself first:

"May I be happy.

May I be peaceful, safe and at ease.

May I be filled with loving presence and loving kindness."

Now send loving kindness to yourself for the next one minute.

While you say these phrases, allow yourself to sink into the intentions they express. After a period of directing loving-kindness toward yourself, bring to mind this other person with whom you want to heal your relationship. Then, slowly repeat phrases of loving-kindness toward them:

"May you be happy.

May you be peaceful, safe, and at ease.

May you be filled with loving presence and loving kindness."

Now send loving-kindness to this person for the next one minute.

Keep doing this for 21 days and you will notice a dramatic softening in your dynamic with this person. Sometimes during loving-kindness meditation, seemingly opposite feelings such as anger, grief, or sadness may arise. Take these to be signs that your heart is softening and revealing what is held there.

Life is a big growth school and our experiences, especially the undesirable ones, are meant to shape us into the divine human beings that we are. We can either choose to focus on our flaws and patterns and release them through deep self-work and mindfulness, or we can choose to stay ignorant and stagnant, and keep inviting the same patterns back into our life.

Allow yourself the gift of evolving and transforming at your own pace, without the added pressure that it should be going any faster or looking different than it does. Don't try to rush the process. Be patient, disciplined and grateful in whatever process you're going through.

The beauty of finally being conscious of the patterns that do not serve you anymore, is that now you get to reclaim your power to rewrite them and choose a new path forward for yourself.

It is important not to confuse breaking open with falling apart. When a pattern that you've held for a long time is coming to an end, that's when you will feel the most discomfort and internal resistance, because being free of it will feel uncomfortable in relation to continuing to play out what you've always known. Change is always hard. Dismantling your old layers to unravel your pure self can be uncomfortable, but everything you want to be is on the other side of it.

Freedom

There is a sunburst in my chest,
A song of haunting glory sweeping like a wave through my body, my
blood, my bones.
The dark veil has fallen from my eyes: Light dances everywhere.
In the clear blue of this sky, there is no room for doubt or pain or fear.
Fear disappears before these rays like fog before rising sun.
My breath is a trumpet of praise, my heart a thunder of gratitude,
Such grace, such gifts, such unbearable ecstasy!
I melt unendingly in an ocean of unconditional love.
My soul gasps in wonder at being ONE, blossoming like a lotus flower
from the roof of my head.
Freedom is a bell resounding in my Being.

IV

RELEASING VICTIM CONSCIOUSNESS

Have you come across someone who is always in a state of sadness, complaint or anger, and when you ask them what's going on, they blame someone, or something else outside of them for being in that state? They feel sorry for themselves, for being the victim of the negative action of others and expect you to feel sorry for them too? Like that friend who is never able to stay in relationships because all the men she encounters only want to clip her wings and take away her sense of identity? Or that relative who continues to blame everyone else in the family for their unfortunate circumstances, without taking any ownership for their own state?

Welcome to Victim Consciousness!

Victim Consciousness is a state of being where you feel that everything, and everyone, outside of you is responsible for what's happening to you. You feel that you are the innocent target of other people's behavior or of your circumstances. You deny all personal responsibility for the things happening in your lives and put the blame on someone else. Nobody likes to admit that they are a victim—at least not consciously. But most of us are susceptible to feeling this way, at some point or another.

Every time you feel slighted, oppressed, unseen, unheard, overlooked, or helpless, realize that you are coming from a place of victim consciousness.

However, this perspective is flawed. Simply because we feel lonely, misunderstood, or hurt, we are, in fact, not a victim. While you continue to believe that you are a victim—helpless, powerless, and ignorant—your life will never change, and you will remain at the mercy of others. Such thoughts are highly disempowering and keep you trapped in a low frequency of blame and complaint.

I have been the poster child for victim consciousness for a long time, so I speak from personal experience. Every time I had a conflict with my partner, or I had a falling out with a friend, I would feel deeply sorry for myself and feel victimized by other people. I would be an equal participant in causing the conflict, yet, I would blame the other person for my misery. Staying stuck in a repeated cycle of drama and conflict for most of my life kept me thinking—in some warped manner—that it was adding depth to my relationships. Of course, I wasn't aware that I was staying stuck in victim mode to attract anyone's attention. I genuinely felt like a victim and was convinced with all my heart that people had been unkind to me. I kept externalizing the causes to either someone or something else.

Shifting blame to something or someone else, for what's going wrong in your life—whether you blame your parents, siblings, boss, partner, community, or circumstances—is a sign of emotional and spiritual immaturity. Being a victim is a safe place as the onus then is on someone else to rescue you. It takes away all responsibility from you to make an empowered choice. To sing the victim song is like saying, "I am stuck here and want to stay stuck here and remain here, forever." It is a losing game.

No one is denying that some of you might have indeed suffered from actual trauma in your life, such as child abuse or domestic violence. In such cases, your experience, your hurt and pain, is valid and real. But it is still your choice not to build an identity around it forever. There is a part of you that likes to hold on to that pain and that memory, and subconsciously you are choosing this self-pity, this pain or suffering, this victim consciousness.

Be aware of your pain, but don't allow it to define who you are. Pain is an emotion that passes. How often do you hold onto these victim stories of what happened to you for several years and build an identity out of it? So much so, that if someone asks you to drop that victim position or move on, you get even more upset or angry with this person. This happens because you feel that they are trying to take away a big part of your identity.

However, in most cases, people have not gone through such extenuating circumstances, and secretly enjoy this feeling of helplessness and stay in victim mode for years or even decades. They may tell themselves, "no one understands me," after one conversation with someone who just wasn't getting them. *Sometimes, they feel wounded for years, if they are not invited, included, or considered by people around them.*

- Let's say, someone at work ignored you and walked past you. How many stories did you just make up in your mind? Maybe that he doesn't like you, he is upset with you, he is competitive with you, he is arrogant, and so on. So many stories go through your mind in that one instant, just to make sense of what happened.

- Maybe your partner forgot your anniversary. What story or narrative did you make up this time? He doesn't care about you, he is self-absorbed, he is unromantic and insensitive.

- Perhaps you were abandoned as a child. What stories did you tell yourself? People abandon you, you are unloved or unworthy of love, it is always your fault—the list can go on and on.

It is not what occurred, but the story that you are giving to what happened, that is hurting you.

Your story is your firmly held beliefs or the narrative that you give to your experiences or to people around you. If you keep holding on to victim thoughts then you will continue to feel overburdened, confused, lacking all personal power. By staying in this loop of self-pity, you will continue to avoid taking responsibility for your life and stay in a pattern of victimization.

You have to do some deep soul searching to realize that, often, it is the interpretation of what happened to you that was hurting you, not the experience itself. Recognizing your stories and how they influence you will make a major shift in your life to becoming self-aware. Catch yourself every time you narrate the events in your life to make yourself out to be a victim. Start by not believing your own thoughts. It is always the interpretation that you give to that event that builds your "story" and you land up creating a sea of suffering for yourself—most times unnecessarily. There is a part of you that feels like a victim and looks for ways to stay in that role. How many times do you exaggerate what one person did to you just to win over another person's opinions? It is not what happened to you, but the exaggerated and lopsided narrative that you give to what happened, that can keep you trapped in victim consciousness, sometimes even for years.

Once we fall into deep victim consciousness, it is hard to rise out of it. In many cases, the victim in one situation becomes the perpetrator in another situation. Without realizing it, the victim begins to play out their own patterns and projections onto others, and, before they know it, they have become perpetrators in other situations.

Some of us thrive in our suffering. Suffering is familiar to all people, but very few of us understand why we suffer. We suffer because we think that there is virtue in suffering—that suffering is needed to find love, to remove guilt, to get attention, to pay for our mistakes, to succeed. Drop this illusion that you _must_ suffer or be a victim or stay a victim in order to achieve anything in life. In fact, the longer you stay in the vibration of suffering, the longer you continue to attract undesirable situations and undesirable people in your life. These events activate what Eckhart Tolle terms our "pain body." We keep this pain body alive by reliving these events and stories in our minds again and again. We keep perpetuating our own pain and suffering and stay in victim mode for years at end.

It is important to question the validity of our thoughts and resist believing all our thoughts. Holding on to our stories can be very depleting to our vital energy and prevent us from feeling complete freedom. We waste a lot of mental and emotional energies in identifying with these stories and lose that pure, soft, innocent, loving, and joyous part of ourselves.

Once you stop creating stories around your emotions, you stop recreating your old identity. Saying things like—no one appreciates me, no one loves me, no one understands me, it's always been this way, it's not my fault, nothing is going to change, I have no choice, I can't change them, it is too difficult to change myself, I feel trapped, he doesn't make me happy, life is against me—are all ways to stay stuck in the victim mode and avoid transformation.

> *Be careful not to validate your own pain so much that you don't make room for your healing.*

Why have you given up your power? How tightly are you holding on to your story? If you cling so tightly to your hurt, you don't make room for your healing. How do you feel when you think about releasing these stories? If you keep identifying with the hurt, you become it. When you, repeatedly and excessively, identify with your hurt or your emotional pain, you forget other happier aspects of yourself, the other experiences living within you, that are buried underneath all that hurt. You need to open up space to honor these other parts of you and release the grip on your victim stories.

You may have invested your identity in the same thoughts and emotions from the past, but, every moment, you are free to choose to not let them define who you are now and let them dissolve and lose their strength over you, with your awareness.

Healing requires us to be honest with ourselves, to see that we are the ones holding on to what is harming us and that we have the choice to let it go and be free.

Every time you are choosing to be a victim, you are making your boss, your colleagues, your partner, your family into a villain. So, if they are the villain, then you are the hero in this. If you are the hero, how can you be a depressed, helpless, and hopeless victim? On a lighter note, that sounds like a really bad movie with a villain and a helpless hero. *An empowered person cannot be a victim.* You have to stop telling yourself, "There is nothing I can do" or, "I have no choice." The first thing to do here is to stop telling yourself that you are trapped as if you are forced or trapped to stay in a job or in a city or in a marriage, for example. Remember, no one can force you into anything.

When you say that 'there is nothing you can do', you are essentially saying that,

a. There is nothing you want to do about it;

b. You are not open to anything else;

c. The other options are too scary.

How is it possible that there is nothing you can do? There is *always* something you can do. You always have a choice, even if it doesn't feel like it. What is required is that you start exercising this *voice of choice*. In some cases, you could really be trapped, like, if you are in a war zone with bombs exploding all around you. But in most other cases, you do have the choice. So, start using the voice of choice. Realize, that even if you are unhappy in a marriage, you are choosing to stay with your partner, maybe out of fear of loneliness, fear of judgment, fear of a financial loss, whatever the reason, but *you are choosing* to stay in that relationship instead of walking away from it. So, you keep trying similar, yet faulty, methods repeatedly to fix your situation, but it doesn't get fixed. When things remain the same, you say nothing works. This is because the core angle from which you are approaching the issue hasn't changed. If you feel like a victim, which is basically hopeless and helpless, then any action you take from this space will give you the wrong result. So, how can your outcome change, *how can the people or situations around you change*?

How do you know if your efforts are working? By checking on the outcome of your efforts. If you are getting the same results as before, then you are resorting to the same faulty methods as before too. You will know that your efforts are in the right direction when the outcomes in your life reflect that change. The day your outcomes change, is when you know that whatever you are doing is working. When you start seeing the results that you want—more peace, harmony, and happiness in your life—you will know you are on the right path.

Remember, nothing is permanent, everything changes. You can rise from anything and completely recreate yourself. You are not stuck.

You always have a choice, so use that voice of choice to tell yourself that you control your own destiny.

Everyone has the capacity to change, as long as there is a willingness to change. Being the victim as a way to get love, sympathy, and attention, is such a powerless place to be in—to feel safe in this helpless cocoon where you don't need to take any responsibility for anything in your life. Your soul wants to fly, to make choices, to make decisions and take ownership of its life, to keep moving. It doesn't like to feel helpless, trapped, or stuck. Only your victim consciousness keeps you stuck in your own trappings.

Ask yourself what needs to change inside you, what needs to shift inside you, so that a completely new possibility or dimension opens up in your life.

Getting Your Inner House in Order

> *You have to begin to tell the story of your life as you now want it to be, and discontinue tales of how it has been or how it was.* —Abraham Hicks

The fruit, when ripe, falls off its own accord. There is no shortcut to ripeness. It happens in its own time. Another word for ripeness is maturity.

How is maturity defined?

When you are mature, you take full and complete responsibility for your own life; when you finally stop passing the buck and realize that you cannot blame anyone or anything else for your state of being and life situation. People who are yet to reach a level of maturity love to blame other people or forces for their own misfortunes and shortcomings. They blame luck, the planets, past lives, parents, spouses, children, bosses, colleagues, the government, karma, God.

Mature people don't do this. They are totally aware and certain that they alone control their inner state, which in turn controls everything that happens in their lives. So, *they learn to focus on tuning themselves, getting their own inner house in order, rather than worrying about anyone else or wasting energy on trying to change other people, places, or circumstances.* They know beyond all shadow of doubt that the *subtle inside* is the *source of all the outside.* Therefore, they understand that they must take responsibility for their own life.

Shifting blame on to anyone outside of you or feeling sorry for yourself is a very disempowered way of being and can cause you to feel depressed. Take charge of your life, start taking responsibility for your choices which led you to this point; take responsibility for your subconscious patterns which attracted these circumstances into your life.

You brought everything into your life, all the wonderful magic of life, as well as all the disasters—it's *all* your doing, they are all self-created issues. Taking responsibility for it will make you feel stronger. It will help you realize that you have the choice to steer your life in a different direction at any time by fine tuning your thoughts, beliefs, and attitude.

What will it take for you to drop your story?

These are our stories—the ones that we create, and live, and relive. If we want to get out of victim consciousness, we need to drop these stories. Sometimes, we may become aware of our stories and their impact and drop them ourselves. And sometimes, we may be able to drop them only with the help of others.

Thankfully for me, my spiritual coach helped to shine a light of awareness on this blind spot and made me aware of my tendency to play victim and stay a victim, as a way of seeking attention and love. (Needless to say, my coach was instrumental in me releasing this pattern from my life.) This book may serve to be a good starting point for you, while you search for that perfect guide to steer you through this.

Try listing all your beliefs and stories. Once you have listed your beliefs about yourself, and identified a few of your stories, look at each one and ask yourself the following 10 questions:

1. Where did this story come from?

2. Is this my story or someone else's?

3. What part of me likes to hold on to this memory or this victim identity?

4. Am I exaggerating what happened to justify my position?

5. Is this story true of me today?

6. Who would I be without this story or this thought?

7. Is this story contributing to, or undermining, my happiness?

8. Is it my experience that's hurting me, or the story that I have given to this experience that's hurting me?

9. What part of my growth and freedom am I blocking by holding on to that story?

10. Am I choosing to continue to live out this story or is it time to write a new one?

Every "story" leads you away from the truth. Answering these questions will point your way to freedom.

Remember, you always have the choice in life to choose a different response and hence, create a new outcome for your life. It is up to you to exercise that choice.

When life forces you into a difficult spot, it is forcing you to drop the victim story and step into your power. Maybe your power being called into question is exactly how you acknowledge and embody your power. Maybe you would have never stepped into your power unless you were forced into that situation. *All the keys to your happiness are with you—when you start believing that you are an empowered being, that you always have a choice, and that you create your own experiences.* When you can see that you have the freedom to choose—a new response to a situation, a new positive attitude—you can begin to break free from this victim mentality. You can think new thoughts, you can create new beliefs, you can feel new emotions. All that matters is you decide and then never look back!

Being powerful and empowered is a complete gamechanger, a new way of being.

Affirmations to heal Victim Consciousness

- *I am not a victim. I am putting the past behind me.*

- *I am not a victim. I stop blaming others and strengthen my relationships.*

- *I am not a victim. I empower myself to take responsibility for my life.*

- *I am not a victim. I choose what happens in my life.*

- *I am not a victim. I attract the care, affection, and respect of others.*

- *I am not a victim. I create and attract everything in my life.*

- *I am not a victim. I am the Master of my life.*

- *I am not a victim. I am peaceful, happy and free.*

Clearing Statements to heal Victim Consciousness

- *I heal any feeling of being a victim, stuck in impossible situations*

- *I release all the ways I used being a victim for punishing others and myself*

- *I release all conscious and subconscious benefits that I may receive by being a victim*

- *I clear all the grief, sadness and other repressed emotions from my mind and heart*

- *I choose to take responsibility for my choices and my experience*

- *I restore all relinquished power, reconnect with my power, make my choices and take actions without fear*

Innocence

Why does the little child touch one's heart?
Because he or she is still innocent.
Innocence is divine because it has not yet been trapped by ego.
The God-spark is still not covered in layers of armor.
Soon, the world will cloak this divine radiance with the mask of the persona.
The original innocence will be buried deep under layers and layers of false selves.
The child will grow into the wary adult—bruised, battered and carefully camouflaged.
Is it possible to return to this innocence?
To shed all the masks, to be naked and pure and radiant again?
The eyes of the sage speak for themselves:
How wonderful—and different—is the innocence that is found again!
Blissful, tranquil and perfect, anchored in the Self forever!

SELF-WORTH YOUR WAY THROUGH LIFE

Self-worth comes from deep acceptance of yourself and a fundamental belief of worthiness. It is knowing that you are whole and complete exactly the way that you are, without needing to prove anything to anyone else. Appreciation and love for yourself are the closest vibrational match to Source or Consciousness you will ever witness in this Universe.

Your soul is a pure, loving, innocent, forgiving, peaceful being of love and light—whole, complete, and worthy exactly the way you are. Even without any professional or financial success, even with your apparent relationship failures, even without perfect health, you are always whole and complete—just the way you are! You are always enough. Anything that prevents you from believing or absorbing this thought is the work of the ego.

> *When you let go of the idea of your limited worth,*
> *you open up space for unlimited possibilities.*

The belief that we are deficient or unworthy in any way keeps us trapped in a trance and each setback in life further exacerbates that feeling of inadequacy. We are always on alert, trying to look for shortcomings in ourselves. We are our own worst critics. So, how do we break this never-ending quest to prove ourselves, to prove our goodness, so that we can feel worthy of all the love and wellbeing in the Universe?

Be Enough for Yourself First

Where do you get your self-worth from? Do you get your identity or self-worth from external things like your job, your bank balance, your assets, your spouse, your network, your family, your friends, your neighbors, your colleagues, your boss, your celebrity friends, your social life, or the followers on your social media? Which of these external yardsticks are you using to measure your self-worth? Who would you be without them?

- Who would you be without your job, your title, your paycheck?

- Who would you be without that seemingly perfect relationship?

- Who would you be without your family name?

- Who would you be without any social invitations?

- Who would you be without your house or cars or those expensive holidays?

- Who would you be without any followers on your social media?

- Who would you be without this body, this face, this appearance?

If you get your identity from one of these external factors, you wouldn't know who you are without them. You will face a deep existential crisis and you could become very depressed and anxious or start feeling empty and worthless from within.

For example, if you get your identity mainly from your work, what happens if you lose your job? What is your first thought? You wonder what your network, family, siblings, colleagues will think of you. *They will only think of you what you think of yourself—they will mirror your thoughts right back to you.* If you take this shift in your circumstances in your stride, then they take the news with grace and ease too. If you judge yourself for it, then that's how they will feel about you too. It all begins with you. Your power is found in choosing the way you interpret and relate with what happens to you.

We don't have to like how it feels when things that define our sense of worth, purpose, or safety dissolve out of sight. And yet loss and change can be honored as spiritual rights of passage, instead of unwarranted moments of cruel misfortune. —Matt Kahn

There is a short, but meaningful, Zen story of a man riding a horse gallantly through the fields, but when asked where he was headed, he said he didn't know—he would ask the horse. The horse was controlling him, instead of him controlling the horse!

This horse symbolizes our habit energy and our chase for materialistic gains and seeking approval from others. The story explains the way we usually live—at the mercy of our old habit energies and mindless activities, not by our intentional actions. The horse is pulling us along, making us run here and there and hurry everywhere, and we don't even know why. If you stop to ask yourself from time to time why exactly you're running around so much, even if you have an answer, it's never a particularly good one. You're just used to being this way, it's how we're taught to live.

Be enough for yourself first. The rest of the world can wait.

For most of us, right from a very young age, we are looking for approval from our family, teachers, or guardians. We continue to carry this need for approval into our adult lives and seek validation from other relationships. When we don't receive this approval, this validation, it diminishes our sense of self-worth.

There is nothing wrong in wanting their approval, as long as your happiness doesn't depend on it. People may or may not understand you completely, they may or may not approve of you, they may or may not support your endeavors. No two people can truly and completely understand each other on this planet, each operates on their own planet of perception. Choose to not let that affect you.

Sometimes, you land up doing a bit too much, be a bit too helpful, give more than you need to, as a subtle way of proving your goodness. Your helpfulness, or your giving, has nothing to do with your "enoughness" or your goodness. You are worthy without needing to do anything to be it. Being helpful or of service is a basic part of being human and being connected to others as a whole, but that does not determine your worthiness. We feel good about ourselves when we are needed by others. However, when you give endlessly just to feel worthy, you have got it backwards. You should give because you have the capacity to give and show up for others when you can, never at your own cost. Never lose yourself to keep someone else. You don't need to overextend yourself to feel worthy, loved, or needed. If you want to feel like 'You Are Enough', you have to start acting like it.

Do not seek to be understood or approved by anyone. You only need to understand yourself, approve of yourself, support yourself. The only person you truly need is you.

Several celebrities, who have seemingly perfect lives, are drawn to end their own life. Some of them link their self-worth to how much they make, some to how famous they are, some to their looks, and some to the number of genuine friends they have and their deep desire to be loved for who they are and not what they have achieved. In some cases, their self-worth comes from the two-three people closest to them in their life, and when they don't receive love or acceptance from these few people, it leads to severe depression. When their source of self-worth is not met or fulfilled, they are pushed to take that unfortunate and extreme step. They forget that their self-worth is not related to their worldly success or their relationships. You don't have to accomplish anything, or hold on to anyone with a tight grasp, to feel worthy.

You can safely assume that getting your self-worth only from yourself is going to be the most significant step in your spiritual journey.

Do you yearn for acceptance and love from your family or friends or relationships? The more you seek validation or approval from others, the more it is going to evade you. Life *will* keep sending people in your life who will not validate you and disapprove of who you are or what you're doing—because it is asking you to transcend this very need to seek validation outside of yourself. It is asking you to learn to validate yourself. You will keep seeking validation or self-worth from other people, until you realize you won't get it from anywhere but your own Being. The *only* person who needs to approve of you, is *you*.

Release the Beggar Mindset

Have you heard the story of the beggar who begged for 30 years in the same spot, sitting on a raggedy, but sturdy, box? Day after day, for thirty years, he sat on the box, asking for alms. He never opened that box because he assumed it was empty all along. One day, a passerby insisted that he open it. To his amazement, he found a treasure of gold inside that chest!

We are all living our lives like that beggar. *We keep looking everywhere for fulfillment, approval, love, peace, happiness—when all these spiritual treasures are waiting to be discovered within our own being.*

Everything you seek already exists in you. A beggar mindset is characterized by a diminished sense of responsibility of one's role in a situation or even one's own circumstances. You are not at the mercy of someone else's opinion of you, or at the mercy of their love and attention, to feel whole again. This is a very disempowered way of being.

You have to take charge of your own happiness and fill the void inside you with your own self-love and self-approval, instead of looking for it from your family, friends, or your partners. Chasing is often about a deeper issue of not feeling loved or lovable; it's a sense of unworthiness inside you, which you think can be filled by someone else's presence in your life. You look to others to fill you up. Until you don't fill that void inside of you, and release this lackness inside of you, no relationship can make you happy. Stop the chase.

Many of us use our relationships to try to fill a void inside of us and when our partners don't meet our expectations, we begin to feel miserable. We become disconnected with ourselves. That's our cue that we need to learn to be happy alone and we need to stop using that relationship to fill the emptiness inside us. The worst move you can make, in response to someone not showing up in your relationship, is to chase or beg them. Chasing your partners for love and attention will only drive them away further. Your neediness will make them even more emotionally unavailable. You have to learn to be whole and happy alone. *If you cannot be happy alone, then you are using that relationship only to fill a void in your life.*

In order to choose someone who doesn't actively choose you, you have to actively stop choosing yourself too—and this diminishes your self-worth.

Stop spending your whole life seeking love, happiness, approval, validation, acceptance. Release this beggar mindset. Stop begging your parents to understand you, for your partners to give you more attention, for your friends to like you, for your bosses to praise you... Stop seeking these things outside of you. The truth is that we will never experience the fullness of life *if we keep looking outside ourselves for the things that we need to seek from within ourselves.*

Realize that you are an empowered being and you can manifest all of your heart's desires. All you need to do is start believing that you are deserving of that happiness, and then demand that the universe give it to you. Your thoughts, actions, and feelings must all align to make you feel worthy of that blessing. That is when you will attract it all into your life.

We believe that only meek and weak people seek self-worth from others. You will be surprised how those we perceive as strong are equally susceptible to this phenomenon. I have chased approval in my own relationships until recently. My father is an extraordinarily successful man who went from being a medical representative in a pharmaceutical company to becoming a CEO. He traveled globally to meet heads of states, other CEOs, and celebrities. He is, by far, the most caring and generous man I know of, and the best father one can ever hope to get. He was my idol and hero growing up, and his approval and appreciation of my professional success and milestones became crucial for my happiness. Any hint of criticism or dismissal from him would trigger my emotional wounds and make me feel incredibly sad. This sadness would then turn into deep disappointment.

The point to focus on here is not of his disapproval itself, but how

I was processing that disapproval for several years of my life. My happiness was at mercy of my father's approval and opinion of me and that was a slippery slope. I had to learn the hard way that I would get his approval only when I stopped seeking it. I had to learn to validate my own self and stop seeking anyone's approval or understanding. I was able to do this with the help of both my spiritual coach and my therapist. They helped me to do some deep clearings and inner child healing work to nurture my inner child back to feeling whole again. Thanks to that work, I have been able to release any blocking thoughts and emotions from my subconscious mind.

Every unmet emotional need comes down to a basic need of being seen or heard. Any lack of being seen or heard in our childhood re-plays out as patterns of seeking this unmet need from our adult relationships. You could be from a very loving, nurturing, and generous family. You may have had the most joyous childhood memories. It is still possible that there were moments in your childhood when you didn't know how to deal with your emotions. Perhaps you were criticized or dismissed and as a child your ability to process these emotions was limited. These wounds will continue to play out into your adult life and turn into patterns, unless you actively seek help to remove these patterns from their root.

We don't crave from others what we have in abundance in ourselves.

When you build enough self-love, self approval, and acceptance you stop seeking it from others. Fill yourself up first. Love yourself first. Know that you are lovable. Somebody else's love or lack of love can never shake this truth. *Don't ever look to others to fill you up—they will never be able to do that and nor should they have to.*

No other person can understand you completely because no one else has walked in your shoes. To be honest, they shouldn't have to understand you. ***It is not their job to like you, it is yours.*** You need to understand yourself, you need to accept yourself, you need to heal yourself, you need to validate yourself.

How do you behave when you need someone's approval? Do you become an inauthentic person and change who you are because you cannot imagine being disapproved of by them? Do you try to say and do things that would please them, even if you don't agree with it? So, what happens even if you do get their approval after all these theatrics? When they begin to like you, they're not liking you, they like the mask that you are wearing, that person you are pretending to be. In seeking their approval, you lose what is genuine and authentic inside of you. You can never get their genuine love this way and you start resenting yourself slowly, too, for being inauthentic.

The search for approval from others is a full-time job assigned to you by your ego. Fire yourself from this role. Stop seeking approval and giving up your power, and start tuning into your intuition to empower yourself.

Validate Yourself

> *Who would you be without the thought that you need anyone's approval?* —**Byron Katie**

If you cannot accept yourself exactly the way that you are, how can others accept you? Any feelings of insecurity and unworthiness emanate when you are disconnected with yourself and who you truly are. It is your connection with Source Energy that reminds you that you are a pure, positive, peaceful soul; an eternal Being of Consciousness that has come to experience this planet and offer unconditional love and compassion to all, starting with yourself.

Instead of becoming a slave for other people's approval or love, start approving yourself. Imagine all the wonderful things about yourself you want to hear from other people. Now, say all those things to yourself in a letter.

- Write a letter to yourself, write down all the things you love about yourself, say all the things to yourself you want to hear from others. Write a letter to yourself as if a friend were to write one to you—full of compassion; one that makes you feel better about yourself, when you don't judge yourself for all your flaws. Let the letter be filled with love, acceptance, forgiveness, compassion, caring, kindness, and connection toward yourself. Read the letter out loud to yourself and let love and compassion take over your being. You deserve it.

Do not mistake this self-approval as an excuse to hide your flaws. If you go around hurting others or being rude to others, that's no reason to be proud of yourself or to continue such behavior. What self-approval teaches us, is to accept ourselves for who we are unconditionally, our strengths and flaws alike. And from this place of deep acceptance begins your journey to work on your flaws. You first accept your flaws without judgment, then work to remove those flaws or those patterns that don't serve you anymore.

Ask yourself this:

- Can I love my depressed self as well as my happy self?
- Can I love my unproductive self as well as my productive self?
- Can I love my uncertain self as well as my confident self?
- Can I love my slowed-down self as well as my active self?
- Can I love my difficult self as well as my easy self?
- Can I love my unlovable self as well as my lovable self?
- Can I love myself exactly as I am?

The fact that you are on this planet, alive, breathing, experiencing life is all you need to feel worthy. Find your connection with yourself, with the divine, with Source, with your Highest Self, with Consciousness and you will automatically feel worthy and loved all the time. As an adult, I have come to realize the universe always wants to give me what I want, I only need to adjust my frequency to catch its blessings. Vibrate at the frequency of gratitude and deservedness, and you will manifest what you are looking for.

Pray and ask for what you desire. Even when you pray, you are sometimes taught in childhood to pray by begging and pleading to God to grant your wishes. When you pray, realize that you are as much of a co-creator with this universe. You are a drop in the ocean of consciousness and every drop makes the ocean what it is. *You are an equal part of the magic and dance in this creation. So, when you pray, you are not only praying to a higher invisible source, you are also lighting up that part of you which is a powerful being that attracts things to itself.* Don't beg, don't chase, just attract things into your life by rewiring your subconscious thinking.

What if life was intentionally putting you through chaos and hardships to ask you to tap into your power:

- To get you to rely on yourself?

- To get your self-worth only from yourself?

- To honor yourself before you honor anyone else?

- To start paying attention to yourself the way you want others to?

- To love yourself completely just the way you are?

- To realize that the only person you truly need is you?

- To know that you are a powerful co-creator in this Universe, and that you choose what you receive and experience in your Universe?

You know that you can be free right away, it is up to you. Start focusing inward and do things that make you happy, that make you feel fulfilled, do things to pamper yourself, validate your own choices and accept yourself completely for who you are. *Act like your presence on this planet is enough for you to deserve all the wellbeing in this world.* You don't need to do all kinds of emotional gymnastics in this life to get people to love you, support you, or notice you. All the love you need is inside you, you only need yourself. Free your mind from the self-created prison where your happiness depends on other people's approval of you. Either you remain forever hungry and thirsty, longing, searching, grabbing, holding, ever losing, and suffering; or you wholeheartedly love and accept yourself and your reality exactly as it is.

It's time. Buy your freedom from yourself.
It's time to Self-Worth your way through life.

Affirmations for your 7 Chakras:

Repeat 3 Times

Focus on each chakra in your body one by one.

- Root Chakra: *I am enough as I am. I am resilient.*

- Sacral Chakra: *I am both sensitive and strong. I have a lot to offer to the world.*

- Solar Plexus Chakra: *I accept myself completely. I build fulfilling relationships.*

- Heart Chakra: *I love and appreciate myself as I am. I love myself unconditionally.*

- Throat Chakra: *I express myself gently and lovingly. I speak my truth.*

- Third Eye Chakra: *I am wise. I am full of potential.*

- Crown Chakra: *I am Consciousness. I am Peace. I am Love. I am Joy.*

Affirmation to Empower Yourself:

Repeat 7 times daily

I am the center of my Universe and I choose what I receive and experience in my Universe.

Thirst

All our lives, no matter what our circumstances or situations are, we are searching, craving—for something to fill the hole, the need deep inside;

Searching for love, for peace, for recognition, for happiness.

We waste days, years, lifetimes looking in all the wrong ways, in all the wrong places.

Stop searching. Stop craving. Drop the need. Drop the needy "I".

That infinite, perfect, ecstatic, loving peace you've been trying to find? It's in you, around you, everywhere.

It's always been there, will always be there. Everything is made of it— nothing else exists!

Only you were the veil, the blockage, the obstacle—the part of you that wants and needs and craves.

The mystic said, "I laugh when I hear that the fish in the water is thirsty."

Drink deep, O fish and become the ocean. Dive deep into the Heart and disappear!

VI

STOP SELF-SABOTAGING WITH ANGER

Anger is the fastest way to self-sabotage! This emotion, originally linked to our survival instinct, helped us face danger, that's why our muscles get tense when we get angry and our heartbeat races faster. However, in today's times, rarely do we face any imminent threat and, yet, some of us use anger as a normal part of our communication. We only get angry because we believe, falsely, that anger works. In reality, it only alienates people, makes them avoid you, pushes the desired outcome away further, causing irreversible damage in our relationships.

All anger and attack are the ego at work, trying to create separation, bitterness and hostility between you and those around you. When we hold onto our anger, we are trying to punish the person who hurt us. But, by doing so, we are hurting ourselves first.

Our first reaction to a difficult situation is often negative. There is a tendency to be carried away in a storm of negative thoughts, which leads us further away from the solution, and eventually leads us to emotional and physical exhaustion. When we get angry and attack, we often make the problems worse, since the other person also feels threatened and attacks in return. Anger acts like poison for our mind, body, and soul. It lowers our vibration and causes severe physical damage to our health including blood pressure issues, heart palpitations, stress, and anxiety.

Anger is a healthy emotion when you need to stand up for yourself or someone else. But when anger becomes a regular response mechanism, it will lead to frequent disruption and dysfunction in your life. That's when anger becomes like poison for us. There is no such thing as righteous anger, it is only a delusion of the ego. Our purpose in life, at all times, is to maintain oneness and not create separation. Even if you feel justified to be upset, you always have a choice to express yourself in a loving, kind, yet, assertive manner without getting angry.

What's hiding behind Anger?

Anger is not always a primary emotion. Often, anger is a derived emotion, a mix of other masked emotions, such as sadness and guilt. When new triggers remind us of past experiences, a mix of sadness, guilt, and shame arise and externalize as anger. Once you understand that these masked emotions are the root cause of anger, you will be filled with compassion for yourself, and for other people who demonstrate anger. You will find it easier to remove your judgments and criticism around anger by understanding what's really hiding behind this anger:

- *Emotional Pain-* Anger is, often, a mask for other hidden emotions like sadness, loneliness, insecurity, feelings of abandonment, or perhaps a need to be seen or heard, to be respected. A strong person gets angry, an emotionally weak person will get sad or depressed. Strong people will mask their insecurities and sadness with anger, as they don't want to expose their vulnerabilities. Strong people are conditioned to believe that being sad makes them appear weak, so they prefer to show aggression or anger instead of sadness. This anger gives them a false sense of control over the situation and prevents them from breaking down. When, in reality, anger-driven by emotional pain, is very often just a cry for attention, a cry for love, a cry to be seen or heard.

- *Guilt-* People also display anger to transfer and deflect feelings of guilt, hurt, and fear on to the other person, since they don't want to experience these feelings in themselves. (We spoke of projection in Chapter 2.) When anger is a mask for guilt, you are only projecting your shame and guilt for your undesirable traits on to the other person. Besides, guilt begets repetition. Which means a guilty person will repeat their mistake just to prove that they weren't wrong for doing it the first time either. You will repeatedly get angry and attack, just to prove to yourself and to others that you didn't do anything wrong in the first place. This further increases guilt in your system, keeping you trapped in an endless loop of attack and guilt.

Real growth happens when you get tired of your own tantrums, your own patterns, and that's when you know you are truly ready to begin your inner transformation. Acknowledging your anger—as unbearable, overwhelming, and exhausting as this process can be—is the only way to release the hold of this energy on your life.

We either manage the discomfort of self-discovery or we manage the discomfort of self-sabotage.

Displaced Anger

What do we do when we are stressed, swamped, or seriously overwhelmed? We unleash our frustration on an innocent bystander. When we cannot unleash our anger on the people we are really angry with, we remove it on a less threatening target who cannot retaliate against us. Perhaps a customer service representative, a cab driver, a server in a restaurant, or our staff? This phenomenon, also known as displaced anger, triggers a series of events in which we make someone else feel worthless, hurt them, cause them to lower their vibration, and make them irritable. They, in turn, express their pain by getting angry at some other unsuspecting target. Before we realize it, we have set off a chain of negative reactions and have polluted this beautiful planet with our negativity.

We *must* realize that we are all ONE, and nothing happens in an isolated universe. We create our own negative karmic footprint when we practice hurtful speech and pollute the world with our negativity. This anger comes back to hurt us at some point in our lives, because every action has its consequences.

Anger isn't always shown by speaking loudly and aggressively. Be alert to the temptation to retaliate passively as well, by giving others the silent treatment or speaking poorly behind anyone's back. Avoid planting this seed of hurtful speech, idle gossip, or other passive-aggressive behavior, as it adds to negative karma in our life, and it will catch up with us. Every time you speak badly about another person, it reveals something that is unhealed within you. If you need to put others down, it comes from a need to put yourself *up*. Resist the temptation to practice such passive aggressive behavior, hurtful speech, and gossip when you are upset with someone, as no one rises by putting another down.

Whatever you are not changing, you are choosing.

Whatever you are not changing about yourself, you are actively choosing to keep alive in your life. Take active interest in transforming yourself and releasing and healing anger. In order to heal anger, you need to heal the sadness behind that anger first. Maybe you have taken genuine steps to release anger from your life such as therapy, meditation, pills, or by being mindful Yet, your anger persists. You might find yourself slipping into your old habit of reacting with anger despite all attempts to eradicate it from your life. In such moments, it might seem like you cannot break this habit and you land up judging yourself even more, every time you get angry. If that happens, don't be overtly hard with— and angry at—yourself. Be patient with yourself, even if you had a weak moment where you regressed to a past habit. Change is not possible overnight. It is enough that you are working on yourself. Don't beat yourself up for not being perfect. We are all just human, accept and embrace your humanness.

Forgive yourself, accept yourself, love yourself, respect yourself, heal yourself, and rise like a phoenix rises from the ashes.

Release any sense of sadness or hopelessness that you feel when you cannot control your anger. Hopelessness is just a story your mind is telling you. It is just an emotion, it will pass. Forgive yourself for not being perfect, forgive yourself for your inability to control your anger—now try again! With consistent efforts and mindfulness, you can release these patterns completely and safely to come to a place of peace.

Anger Clearing Affirmations

Repeat 7 times each

For as many days as you need to say it:

I clear all the ways I become angry with others.
I clear all the ways I am angry with myself.
I clear all the ways I get frustrated.
I clear all the ways I am sad underneath this anger.
I clear all the ways I feel guilt underneath this anger.
I clear all my judgments related with my anger.

Guilt Attracts Self Punishment

Guilt shows up for so many reasons, sometimes it shows up as a way for us to stay attached, of holding on to someone we lost maybe because of our actions.

Guilt is a wasted emotion. Even if you believe you did something that was truly wrong, remind yourself that you cannot rectify the past, you can only learn from it and create a new future. If you carry guilt, it gnaws at you, lowers your frequency and attracts punishment. The Universe wants us to learn, grow, and move on, not stay stuck in our guilt.

There are several studies that prove that guilt attracts self-punishment. If you carry a guilt-ridden consciousness you will attract situations in your life to punish yourself for your "wrongdoings". *When deeply internalized, the consciousness of guilt energetically attracts punishment.* When you feel guilty about something, you feel ashamed, you don't feel deserving of good things in your life, no matter what people offer you. These feelings of un-deservedness are often deep-rooted and potent; leading to anger, frustration, and self-loathing. This self-loathing attracts self-punishment into your life, because deep down you feel that you deserve to pay for what you did. The Universe matches your frequency. Regret is a more effective emotion than guilt, as regret is based on a desire to change the part of you at its core, that caused that mistake in the first place.

You *can* break free from this cycle. One of the ways to do so is by practicing self-restraint. Each time you practice self-restraint, you win. A therapist can also guide you quite effectively to heal this emotion.

As a child our ability to discern a right response from a hurtful response is low, so we absorb everything around us like a sponge. If during childhood, we were around parents or other people with anger issues, our subconscious mind was recording that experience as an acceptable response mechanism. Without realizing it, we grew up reacting in *that* exact manner. As a child you might have thought that you will never be like this angry person. You, however, might still grow up embodying anger issues because your subconscious mind recorded that behavior as an acceptable way to express yourself. It's time to unlearn that behavior. It's time to forgive yourself for having this trait. And while you're at it, forgive the people who taught you to be angry, for they didn't know any better either. Because not forgiving has its costs. When we keep grievances and hold grudges, we retain the anxiety, irritability, anger, depression, lack of trust—the list is long and full of despairinside our mind and heart. *Do you really want to choose to keep all that? Probably not.*

Anger Clearings based on Access Consciousness©

Repeat 7 times each

For as many days as you need to say it:

"In all the ways—consciously or unconsciously—that I have picked up patterns of anger from anyone in this lifetime or across lifetimes, space, and dimensions, I send it back to the universe and delete, destroy, and uncreate it all, wherever I have made it mine. POC POD POC POD POC POD"

POC: Is the point of creation of the thoughts, feelings and emotions immediately preceding whatever you decided.

POD: Is the point of destruction immediately following whatever you decided. It's like pulling the bottom card out of a house of cards. The whole thing falls down.

As someone who has struggled a lot with anger in the past, I can empathize with those who struggle with it. I would get angry to express myself, when the truth was that I was feeling sad or hurt.

Because I did not want to show my vulnerability, expose my sadness, or show that I was hurting in any way, I would prefer to demonstrate anger. If someone said something that would hurt me, I would counterattack immediately and say hurtful things, only to feel immense guilt just moments later. I allowed their words to control my emotions. I saw this pattern manifest very frequently in all my relationships, both professional and personal. While I am known to be a loving and compassionate person, my anger used to be my Achilles heel, making people want to keep a 'safe' distance from me. That is how I began my spiritual journey, when I realized that I was sabotaging my own life with my anger. With the help of some spiritual therapy, bit by bit, I released it from my life.

As can you. You only need to acknowledge it and be willing to heal it.

The distance between who you are and who you want to be is only separated by what you do.

As spiritual seekers, and you are one else you wouldn't be holding this book, we hold ourselves to higher standards. So, while we are working on ourselves to release our anger, it is imperative to be compassionate toward ourselves. While you are working on this inner transformation, it is likely that anger will keep resurfacing. Don't allow yourself to get disappointed and give yourself more reasons to judge and reject yourself. *Make sure you are developing self-compassion as much as self-awareness.* This will give you the space that you need to make a different choice when something new, different, or even similar upsets you. Develop a new relationship with anger—one of understanding, compassion, acceptance, and forgiveness.

Healing happens in layers, not all at once. Sometimes, the situation keeps coming up until all the charge around that trigger has healed.

Healing Anger

There are multiple ways to heal anger. One of the ways is to practice mindfulness. *The ability to observe, without reacting, is what allows—and helps—us to stop recreating the past.* You are welcome to express your views, to disagree with others. Try to do so without any emotional charge, without attack and blame. Change the mental and emotional energies with which you express yourself during a disagreement. Take the emotion, the charge, the attack away and then express yourself calmly and objectively. Anger is effective when it is expressed with direct, clear, honest words about the issue and how it is making you feel, versus attacking the person who triggered the anger. This will help the other person to not take the feedback personally and inspire them to change.

Whenever you feel anger arise in you, close your eyes and do this quick exercise for a few minutes:

Imagine a miniature version of you (which embodies the part of you that is angry) inside your heart—angry, attacking, vindictive. Now shine a white light of consciousness, love, and peace on this miniature you and imagine becoming completely peaceful. Now imagine another miniature version of you which embodies the part of you that is sad and hurt. Once again, shine this white light of consciousness on this part of you. Feel the peace that starts to emanate from your Being. Open your eyes, slowly, and observe how you are feeling. You will find yourself calmer than before. Now, go back and respond to the situation at hand, calmly and gently.

If you want to take your spiritual growth to the next level, you can use these undesirable situations of conflict not just to change yourself, but also to transform the other person. How is that even possible? At the onset or during a conflict, you can make a conscious decision of how you want to interact with the other person. Drop your ego, drop the negativity, soften your expression and keep your body language open and engaging. Then express yourself in a heartfelt manner with love and authenticity to explain your point of view. Offering them this respect and grace in your response— even when they are disrespecting you—will soften them and make them drop their armor too, as they will feel less threatened in your presence. By doing this, not only do you manage to de-escalate the situation, but also transform the dynamic to one of mutual respect.

Go a step further, close your eyes and send them a white healing light for 20 seconds and forgive them for hurting you. Forgiving them heals you.

Forgiveness Buys Your Freedom

Forgiveness is the perfect antidote to anger. When you forgive, you empty your mind of all the unpleasant feelings which have made you their prisoner. When you forgive, you buy your own freedom from anger. If you find it hard to forgive others, you probably find it hard to forgive yourself too. *The relationship you have with others is always a reflection of the relationship you have with yourself.* So, start by forgiving yourself for all the times you hurt others consciously or unconsciously with your words, thoughts, or actions. Then start forgiving others too.

The relationship you have with yourself is the most complicated one because you cannot walk away from yourself. You have to forgive every mistake. You have to deal with your own flaws. You have to find a way to forgive yourself first, in order to forgive another with all of your heart.

We make others pay for the same mistake multiple times. As author Don Miguel Ruiz says, *"Every time we remember someone's mistake, we blame them again and send them all the emotional poison we feel at the injustice, and then we make them pay again for the same mistake."* How is that fair?

Forgiving others is important for you, not for the other person. We can even forgive someone without letting them know.

Forgiveness frees up our energy for other things. When we hold on to resentment, hurt or pain, we lose something sweet and innocent inside us, and it depletes our own vibration. It also ruins our health and creates long term triggers inside us which make us defensive, or aggressive, or both, and keeps us locked in the memory of a past moment which serves no purpose to our present.

True Forgiveness is the greatest gift you can give yourself.

Can you try to forgive even the worst of your 'enemies'—people who have hurt you intentionally? An enemy doesn't have to be *literal*. An enemy can be *anyone* who doesn't live up to your expectations, who lets you down, who doesn't do what you tell them to do, and, in a sense, who stands against you for some reason or another.

Can you forgive them, even if they have not apologized yet? Think of them as children who are unaware of what they are doing, unaware of their own spiritual malaise or the negative karmic footprint that they are creating. Forgiving is *not* pretending that nothing happened. It is, instead, about focusing your energies on fixing your own inner state, rather than expecting that the other will change. Go inward and see where you are holding on to resentment and let it go. No one is asking you to bring anyone back into your life or to continue to tolerate bad behavior from them. Just to forgive them and buy your freedom from this prison of resentment. *Lasting transformations happen when we remove our attention from trying to control the external world and invest our energy in improving our own response and state of being.*

If you are expecting an apology from others, sometimes we must accept that the acknowledgement, witnessing, or apology is going to come from someone other than the person we desperately want it from. Make room for that. Our healing is not person-specific. To be seen and understood in a transcendent way can be done by others.-Vienna Pharaon, Therapist

Can you go a step further and pray for their happiness? We all pray for our friends and family, that is common. Real spiritual heights are attained when you can truly forgive and wish well, even for those who stand against you.

Here is one effective way to do that–

Think of 3 people who have hurt you the most and send them white healing light. Imagine their whole body filling up with Divine white light, cleaning their heart, mind, and soul. Do this for 30 seconds per person. You will feel much lighter and happier in a matter of minutes. Do this as often as you need to.

Spiritual growth is all about unconditional love for all. The first step to feeling unconditional love for all is to forgive everyone who has harmed you. Love is a powerful gift that opens up hearts and melts resistance. Love is a great neutralizer, deflector, and reflector. So, forgive those who have "wronged" you. Forgive yourself, forgive your family, forgive your friends, forgive the unkind stranger on the street, the rude waitress, forgive everyone who has ever brought you to pain or sorrow. Forgiving people raises your own vibration and brings you to a space of peace. Spirituality is a choice in every single moment of your life. What will you choose?

The key to creating everlasting change on this planet, is to create everlasting peace within yourself.

When you do that you return to your divinity, to love, to peace. You come back home. When you cross this barrier within you, there is a deep opening in your heart.

Affirmations to clear Anger and Guilt

Repeat 3 times.

For as many days as you need to:

- *I release all the memories and thoughts that perpetuate guilt and self-judgment.*

- *I release any justification and subconscious advantages in holding on to guilt.*
- *I release all conscious and unconscious patterns of self-sabotage and self-punishment.*
- *I release all grievances against others.*
- *I release any sense of shame and unworthiness.*
- *I release my misperceptions.*
- *I release the desire to blame and punish others.*
- *I release the constant state of tightness, tension, and anxiety the game of attack and defense keeps me in.*
- *I release the desire to attack anyone and the defensive structures created out of fear.*
- *I choose joy instead of proving my rightness; and gratitude instead of guilt.*
- *I choose peace and forgiveness and allow myself to receive the ever-present grace.*

The Source

Water from a deep mountain spring is clear and sweet and good.
Water from a dirty drain is filthy and poisoned.
Its purity depends upon its source.
Life is a continuous stream of thoughts, feelings and actions.
By themselves, these are neither good nor bad.
What matters is: are they effective, are they useful, do they improve the quality of your existence?
This depends on where they come from, the source.
If they come from unconsciousness, from the layers of unawareness, they are polluted and ineffective: all they do is create additional negativity.
If they come from conscious awareness, from ever-present Being, they will be effortlessly elegant, positive, creative and beneficial to you and all around you.
Seek the right source: then all your actions will be spontaneously perfect always.

THE LAW
OF POLARITIES

A Polarity is a relationship between two opposite characteristics or tendencies that exist in the same person. A polarity, in a spiritual context, is the representation of areas of consciousness that appear to be opposite to one another. For example, without experiencing hot, how would you know what it feels like to be cold? Without sadness, could you really know and appreciate the feeling of happiness? In effect, they are each two components of the same body of consciousness, just with a different focus.

If everything has an opposite, that also means that

a)   Everything in life is of a dual nature, because when it comes to opposites, you cannot have one without a potential for the other, and;

b)   Two opposites, while being completely different, will always exist on the same plane of being.

There is always a potential for the opposite, because neither one can stand alone. This means that *both experiences must come together to make one whole experience.* Even if you separate something into two completely opposite parts—each of those parts still contains the potentiality of the other.

What that means is that these polarities exist in our thoughts and feelings as well. A loving person can also be an angry person, a victim can also be a perpetrator, a mature person can also behave childishly. We have polarizing thoughts, opinions, feelings on many topics in our life. You can even choose to act out one polarity one day and another polarity the next. You will land up acting out the polarity that has a stronger pull on you in any given moment.

When our pendulum is pulled heavily in one direction, it will want to swing to the other extreme to bring a sense of balance to our being.

The more we choose to act out one extreme, the more we are pulled in the opposite direction. We land up acting out the polarity that feels the strongest in that moment. For instance, if you have spent a majority of your life shouldering responsibilities, then you will want to break free and become carefree. If you grew up with a very strict and controlling parent, then you will crave all the things you were stopped from doing.

Hence, staying in our equilibrium and trying to maintain—at the very least—a semblance of a balance is key. Each one of us will have a different equilibrium; and that's ok. The less we act out our extremes, the less energy we spend on moving from one extreme to the other. The more we stay centered in our own equilibrium, in our Tao, the greater is our ability to move forward in life. While that may sound like just basic physics, it's true for us as well, because at the end of the day we are all just pure energy. This is what is called the *Pendulum Effect of Extremes.*

Here's the main thing to understand about the Law of Polarity:

- *It tells us that there is always a positive for every negative in our life. If we want to manifest more of the positive, we need to consciously seek it out, even in the midst of a negative situation.*

- *The Law of Polarity gives us the confidence that the positive is always there, even if you can't see it. It's there because it has to be there. Nothing in this universe exists without its opposite.*

To really use the Law of Polarity in your life requires focus. It's very easy to get carried away with our emotions when bad things happen. Sometimes, the positive won't be easy to see, so you'll have to be determined to find it. As you begin to understand and embrace the Law of Polarity, it will soon become second nature to look for the opposite in every circumstance that arises.

Just know that all paradoxes within us can be reconciled. All polarizing energies can be harmonized. We are all a combination of divine and human qualities, of masculine and feminine energies, of good and bad qualities. When we realize this, we can own both our divinity and our humanity.

Balancing Masculine-Feminine Energy

We also have masculine and feminine polarities inside us—the yin and the yang—and often we struggle to bring them to harmony. These dual energies are an intrinsic part of us and in everything around us. We all lead from the dominant energy inside of us, regardless of our gender. Let's try to understand these dualities inside of us and how we can balance them to live a happy life.

Balanced feminine energy is intuitive, loving, compassionate, patient, healing, still, creative, truth-seeking, connected with nature, whole, self-assured, empowered, sexual, and abundant. With this sacred feminine energy, you can make intuitive, heart-based decisions, and feel and move with the flow of life. This energy commands respect, can be strong and assertive, and knows where to draw boundaries without being abrasive, without hurting others.

On the other hand, the *unbalanced feminine* is overly sensitive, too empathetic, needy, co-dependent, insecure, manipulative, depressed, self-doubting, and has low self-esteem. We often mistake feminine energy to be weak because we associate the stereotypical woman with this unbalanced feminine energy.

The *balanced masculine* energy is powerful, strong, supportive, protective, energized, physical, confident, focused, and active. It is independent, free, fast, logical, analytical, and courageous.

The *unbalanced masculine* is an arrogant, egotistical, headstrong, stubborn, and relentless energy; disconnected from emotions, often going into overdrive, and not resting. Unbalanced masculine energy can be destructive, with a tendency to self-sabotage relationships.

One person can embody the characteristics of all four polarities mentioned above. For example,

- Strong, independent women—especially urban women—

overdevelop their masculine energy and feel that they need to act in aggressive or dominant ways to get things done around them. In this bargain, they minimize the role of their balanced feminine energy. They start to exude masculine energy, in the name of confidence, which is often unnecessary. Everything is vibrational, everything is energy. Women don't need to become aggressive or masculine to get things done. They can achieve their goals by standing firm in their balanced feminine energy. In fact, this approach is often much more effective. To be who you were born to be. Balanced feminine energy.

- Alternatively, if you often feel worn out from always taking on other people's energy, if you feel resentful, insecure, disempowered and lonely, that is an indication that you have to reduce the unbalanced feminine energy and need to tap into more of your masculine energy.

- Some urban women in their thirties and forties embody aspects of both balanced and imbalanced masculine and feminine traits. They check all four boxes. I know women who can be strong, independent, and decisive at work, yet, could be very needy and insecure in their personal life. They can literally go from one extreme of being aggressive and direct, exposing their imbalanced masculine traits; to crying and feeling insecure and needy for love and attention, the same day. I have active conversations with women in healing circles and therapy groups who are very aware that they need to balance their masculine-feminine polarities and bring them into harmony.

Equally, many men suffer from an imbalance of masculine energy.

As they are denied their expression of the feminine, they are unable to be vulnerable and emotional, and, instead, overdevelop their masculine in an unhealthy way. Do you feel overworked and burnt out? Do you move through life without thinking, on autopilot? Are you always doing and striving, without really feeling emotionally connected to your goal? Do you feel you lose your cool easily on others and feel frustrated and angry? That indicates a need to release some of that imbalanced masculine energy.

However, when these traits or habits are deeply ingrained, it is extremely difficult to unlearn these habits without professional help. We pick up these tendencies at a young age from our parents or guardians, which can be released with the help of hypnotherapy or talk therapy.

I have outlined one such self-hypnosis technique below.

Let's work on a hypothetical situation. Let's say you picked up a high degree of imbalanced masculinity from your father, which made you controlling or angry. You picked up a high degree of imbalanced femininity from your mother as well, which made you needy, overly sensitive, or codependent in relationships. This self-hypnosis technique can help you return the energies you picked from them and balance your polarities a lot better.

- *Lie down on your bed, close your eyes, count down slowly in your mind from 10 to 0 to calm yourself.*
- *Now, imagine you are standing in a plain room with white walls. Invite your parents in this room with you.*
- *Now, invite both the masculine part of you and the feminine part*

of you into the room. Imagine two different parts of you walking into the room.

- *Slowly return all the masculine energy you received from your father to him. From the masculine part of you, imagine a smoke or light leaving you and returning to him and say, "I am not you and I return this anger and control to you".*
- *Wait till the energy has completely left you.*
- *Now, do the same with your mother. Imagine your feminine side returning the unbalanced feminine traits that you learnt from her. Imagine a smoke or light leaving you and returning to her. Repeat the same words we used above. "I am not you, I return this neediness and insecurity back to you"*
- *Wait till the energy has completely left you.*
- *Now, thank your parents for their time and give them the permission to leave the room.*
- *Now, integrate both your masculine and feminine energies into a big ball of white light. Now, integrate this white light inside you. Feel the lightness and the ease.*
- *Now, bring yourself back to where you are now, in this moment.*
- *Then open your eyes slowly and say,*

"I am in balance. I am in balance. I am in balance. Equilibrium Restored."

Do this for seven days and feel a tremendous transformation and shift inside you.

(You can replace your parents with anyone else and replace the traits you want to clear with the ones you are looking to release. The above therapy is just one example.)

Other effective ways to balance out our extremes or our polarities is to listen to guided meditations, meditate, journal, sleep, give, volunteer, or practice random acts of kindness. Give back to yourself first and foremost, take care of yourself, carve out time for self-care, and bring yourself into balance. All polarities can be reconciled and brought into balance.

The Song of You and Me

When you are me,
And I am you,
And we are nothing flowing into everything,
Who can speak of "love "or "gratitude" or "giving" or "receiving"?
Contentment is drinking tea
And watching the sky
And wondering at the everchanging masterpiece
Reflected in the everchanging Eye
Of the Divine Artist
Who is the painter and the painting?
the sculptor and the statue, the singer and the song.
Is this deep peace not our home, where we truly belong?
Love overflows like an endless ocean that reaches every shore
And the greatest wisdom is to truly know nothing anymore.

So what is there to do or say? Just be!
And flow like a river gentle to the sea.
This is the sweet dance of you and me.

PART 2

RISING HIGHER

VIII
UNLEARNING
TO RELEARN

Life, sometimes, isn't about becoming something as much as it is about unbecoming everything that you are. This entails shedding all the layers of your ego, to drop your strongpoints of view, your opinions, your complaints, your demands, your biases, your negativity, your anger, your need for control, your grievances. We have to identify all the layers that we have to shed.

We are on an inevitable course of awakening. We start from innocence and we return to innocence. *A soul takes human birth in order to have a series of experiences through which it will awaken out of its illusion of separateness.* If you understand this, you will engage with your spiritual practices from a place of patience and timelessness.

We must admit that some of the ways we approach situations in life, like our relationships, come in part from our parents. We all grow up witnessing our parents' interactions with each other, and for better and worse, a lot of that sticks with us all the way into adulthood. As children, our mind is like a sponge absorbing everything, including these habits or patterns from our parents, without any conscious thinking.

We then, subconsciously, seek romantic partners, who seem like our parents, to repair our parental relationships. We expect to receive from these partners that which we didn't receive from our parents. We might even see the same red flags in them as we did in our parents. Then we embark on a journey of fixing the relationship— despite the red flags—because these red flags feel like 'home'. You learnt from your parents what a relationship should look like. You now continue to play out their patterns in your relationship as well. Not just your love relationship, but all your adult interrelationships will be a byproduct of how you watched your parents interact and respond to the world.

For example, if you were conditioned to neglect, abandonment, or an emotionally absent parent, then you may have learnt to perform to get love and attention. You will grow up thinking you always need to *do* a lot in your relationships to receive attention; and you might overcompensate for someone else not showing up in your relationships.

The first step to healing this part of yourself is to acknowledge that you have imbibed certain response mechanisms, which continue to cause conflict and drama in your life, which need to be unlearned. This is the hardest part to do, and, yet, the most vital step in your journey to self-heal. The more you resist acknowledging that you have incorporated their traits, the more these traits become ingrained in you. That which you resist, persists.

We have been programmed to learn certain behaviors from birth.

Like how to get attention from people, how to talk to others, how to express love, whether to be hardworking or lazy, to chase people for approval or seek it from oneself, to chase material success or inner peace, and so on. All these belief systems, habits, and attitudes get deeply ingrained in our mind simply by observing our parents, or teachers around us at a very young and impressionable age. In order to seek their approval, we become like them and imbibe their belief systems *without conscious thought*, such as their religious beliefs, racial beliefs, money beliefs, relationship beliefs, and even their communication styles!

As daughters, we may inherit a lot of our beliefs and sense of self-worth from our mothers. I inherited the belief that as women, we need men to approve and validate our every move, and what they think of us is of paramount importance. I have actively worked on unlearning this pattern in my life.

We grow up blindly following our parent's belief systems, without questioning their validity. Even as adults, we act and respond to life in ways that would please them, since we are constantly trying to look for their approval. We are so accustomed to wanting our parent's approval since we are infants that we don't even realize that we have been playing this approval game from our childhood to this present day.

To find your own truth, your own beliefs, you have to question if what you learned is contributing to your happiness, does it work for you, or is it time to release it now?

What have you imbibed from your parents, your guardians, your teachers, which you no longer want to keep in your life?

A large part of your growth will involve unlearning these things you learnt consciously or subconsciously from your parents or guardians you grew up with. Your parents might be very loving and well-meaning people, which might make this process even more of a challenge for you. Your parents are, after all, human. They have their strengths and their flaws, their prejudices and their projections, none of which makes them terrible people. It only makes them limited ones—just like the rest of us!

Don't forget that you are powerful and capable of ending these cycles, old stories, and patterns. The path is not easy, but you are a resilient and wise being. You can do the work needed to break free and unlearn what you learnt unknowingly while growing up. The only person who can save you is yourself. You're allowed to rewrite the patterns and belief systems that were passed down to you. You're allowed to reclaim your own identity now.

The best work we can do for all our relationships is the work we do on ourselves.

Access Consciousness© Clearing Statements

Repeat 7 times each

For as many days as you need to say it:

"All the ways, knowingly or unknowingly, consciously or unconsciously, I have picked up patterns of {neediness, anger, defensiveness, complaining} from my {mother, father, sibling, teacher} or from anyone else in this lifetime, or across lifetimes, space, and dimensions, I send it back to the universe and delete, destroy, and uncreate it all wherever I have made it mine. POC POD POC POD POC POD"

POC: Is the point of creation of the thoughts, feelings, and emotions immediately preceding whatever you decided

POD: Is the point of destruction immediately following whatever you decided. It's like pulling the bottom card out of a house of cards. The whole thing falls down.

Childhood Trauma

We often correlate childhood trauma with verbal, physical, or sexual abuse; or even abandonment issues, if your parents walked out on you at a young age. What we don't realize is that childhood trauma also includes experiencing a parent who denies your reality, who doesn't acknowledge or see you for who you are, who stops you from feeling certain emotions, who berates you or makes you feel like a disappointment all the time, or one who cannot balance and regulate their own emotions. In some cases, being made to feel guilty, every time you fell short of their expectations, could have been traumatic to a child who wanted to fulfil his/her own dream. What's traumatic depends on how you internalized these issues as a child. If you had well-meaning and supportive families, for the most part, and parents who did a lot for you, you can be shamed by others or by yourself for having such feelings of disappointment toward your parents. You can land up feeling very confused by your feelings toward them and you might land up avoiding your healing if you do not acknowledge these wounds.

We need to be able to recognize and acknowledge our own truths. You don't need to explain these to others, it is more important to recognize these things yourself. Truth within is a deep understanding of the self that doesn't need to be explained externally, the knowing within is enough. You don't need your parents or guardians or other members of your family to recognize it.

In fact, the externalizing of your truth sometimes may loop you back—into unhealthy cycles with a person who is committed to misunderstanding you to protect themselves. Think about your experience as a child, when your parents just couldn't validate your experience, even though you were not trying to hurt them. Or perhaps you have been around a gas-lighter—someone who is highly committed to manipulating you, via psychological means, into doubting yourself, to protecting themselves and/or to being in control. But, you must still realize these truths and these experiences for yourself. Instead of letting them hurt you through unconscious identification and emerge as unhealthy patterns in your life, let them become the entry point for expansion, boundaries, and deep healing. What you know to be true is enough. You don't need to prove this to anyone else.

When our parents didn't show us how to emotionally regulate or process difficult emotions, we began to cope by taking on different roles—that of a caretaker, or the rescuer, or the one who is always available for others at the cost of neglecting oneself. Perhaps it is time to stop now. You are deserving of relief. Of that weight being lifted off your shoulders. You are not meant to carry or absorb the burden of your family problems, and their disappointments with one another, or the weight of your family secrets. You were not meant to act or behave like an adult when you were just a child.

Trauma can go unrecognized for several years, until you take charge of your own pain. When you do, you tell yourself it is ok to love your parents and, at the same time, realize you have also suffered at their hands without blame, resentment, and accusations. Inner Child Healing Therapy can help to heal this child inside you and support and nurture that child back to feeling whole again.

Healing your inner child to release any childhood trauma starts by seeing yourself, hearing yourself, forgiving yourself, accepting yourself, and loving yourself just the way you are. Offering love to the parts of yourself that you've kept hidden, quiet, or curled up, is a radical act of self-love and accepting your humanity. We don't have to have a perfect relationship with ourselves in order to be receptive to our own love.

The beauty of offering love to ourselves is that we don't need to feel lovable or like every part of ourselves before we choose to do so.

You are allowed to unlearn who you've been—if it's not who you are anymore.

You are here to find your own journey toward healing and walk your own path.
You are allowed to redefine yourself.
You are allowed to change your mind.
You are allowed to make a big transition.
You are allowed to shake things up.
You are allowed to unlearn who you've been, to become who you want to be.

We are conditioned, to stay the course and root for stability, and not make room for change easily, by society. But sometimes we realize that the things we signed up for once—a behavior, an attitude, a belief, a job, a relationship—just isn't for us anymore. We realize that our ideas, our dreams, our visions have shifted, which means we shift how we show up in the world and how we interact with this world.

It's time to start cleaning the many layers of dirt from the original spotless mirror.

The human condition is both poignant and mysterious—filled with pleasure and pain, with great promise and deep anguish, with peaks of triumph and valleys of failure, with despair and delight. It is the dance of the opposites amidst the inevitability of endings, that makes this life so magical!

Unlearning

I thought learning was difficult.
All those years of studies, reading, learning.
Now I find what is really difficult is un-learning:
Getting rid of all the concepts, all the clever dialogues, discussions,
interpretations;
Cleaning the many layers of dirt from the original spotless mirror.
Why is that difficult?
If I have covered myself with an armor built of multiple layers of mud,
why can't I just clean it off?
Only because I have allowed it to become my identity, the shell that I
fondly cling to-
I am afraid that removing it would leave me exposed and vulnerable
like a new-born baby.
How strange!
Humans would rather cling to their armor of personality, even if they
are aware that it is the source of all their misery, than be conscious,
blissful and free!

IX
HEALING THROUGH DEPRESSION

Depression is a complex topic, with so many layers that there is no one-size-fits-all cure for it. Healing yourself of depression requires healing through many complex layers, through persistent self-work, to explore your shadows with an open mind.

For some, depression could be genetic or hormonal, for some it could be related to a specific event in their life—such as the loss of a loved one, and for some, it could simply be a strong resistance and inability to accept what is. Depression could also be a sign that you are not happy with the choices you have made in life. That you are leading a life that is not in tune with your integrity or your expectations, in which case, depression could simply be the outcome of a dishonest life.

While depression plays out as an emotion, it reflects in your physical energy as well. It leaves you with a constant feeling of despair, making you believe, falsely, that you might be permanently broken.

Depression has both a) a physical side, and b) a mental-emotional-spiritual side to it, and in order to heal completely, you need to address both aspects of depression.

Depression is a physical thing. It is physiological. A hormonal upheaval. A snag in the brain, caused by hormonal or genetic imbalances, also known as chemical depression. Many fail to realize or accept this fact. It is important to curb this physical aspect, this chemical reaction, first, and then you can deal with the mental-emotional energies in a more effective manner.

Allopathic solutions can be effective to curb physical depression. You might be resistant to taking help because it is difficult to acknowledge to yourself that you might be broken or that you need help. All the advice in the world will not help you until you help yourself. You have to overcome this taboo and remove your judgment associated with mental health issues in your own mind first. Acupuncture is also an effective alternative therapy to control physical or chemical depression. *Accepting or acknowledging that you need help is an act of self-love and immense courage.* Healing the physical side of depression first helps to control the overflow of emotions which can then free up a lot of mental-emotional energies for you to deal with the issues at hand, either by being more mindful yourself, or by taking traditional or spiritual counselling to talk through your problems with a professional. However, it is imperative that you address the physical side of depression first.

Now let's talk about the mental-emotional-spiritual aspect of depression.

The book, *A Course in Miracles*, will tell us that we are living in a dream and all of this is an illusion. If all of this is an illusion, created by our egoic mind, then we are all sleeping, and this is all just a dream. *Depression is a sign that you have made something or someone very significant in this dream, more significant than your own peace and happiness.*

Ask yourself, what have you made so significant in this dream?

What have you made so important to your existence, that not having it is causing you so much sadness now? A relationship, a job, someone's approval? Only you can drop the significance you have attached to that dream and accept reality for what it is, with grace. You create your own illusions and delude yourself that these illusions will make you happy. Then you make it worse by insisting that these illusions must go your way and when they don't, you enter this hole of depression.

Release all these delusions, these distortions of the mind, because they are nothing more than a tribute to your ego. *The ego fears nothing more than its own annihilation.* We stay trapped in these distorted thoughts and make them particularly important to our existence, which serve as an escape to disguise the emptiness within us. They give us something to think about, complain about, lament about, and add to the delusions of our mind.

If something bad happens to us, we will inevitably feel pain in the moment. But, after the misfortune's initial impact we prolong our suffering by brooding over what happened, reliving our pain and continuing to feed the wound of the initial impact.

• Imagine if you get struck by an arrow, it would be very painful.

- Now imagine being struck by a second arrow, that would be even more painful, isn't it?

That first arrow is the painful triggering event in our life which we cannot control. However, the second arrow is our reaction to the first, *our self-created suffering* for prolonging our misery by resisting what happened. With this second arrow comes the possibility of choice. The saying, 'Pain is inevitable, suffering is optional', is illustrated perfectly through this example.

Let's distinguish between pain and suffering. Pain is biological and impersonal, but suffering is psychological and requires a sufferer. Without craving or resistance, there is no suffering. Feeling the feeling is one thing, getting caught in a story about what these feelings mean is another. That is called suffering.

Resistance or dramatization of pain are both just self-inflicted emotional wounds.

Things are never as bad as they seem. It's the story (or the narrative) that you are giving to the situation, which makes it a "good" or "bad" event. Depression or stress is a sign that you are struggling with reality, that you are denying reality, and that it is nothing more than your resistance or inability to accept what is.

For example, if you get laid off from work, and you go into depression because of that; or if someone breaks up with you and you tell yourself you are depressed—these are all just self-created delusions, to hold onto your victim consciousness. What good will it do to deny or resist reality? You can either go through these events in life kicking and screaming and prolong your pain or accept them with grace and ease. The choice is yours.

People and things come and go, for such is their nature. They come into our life when we need them and when we no longer need them, they are gone. How do you know you no longer need them? When you see they are not there anymore, that's how. *Reality is always kind and shows us what we need and what we don't. Things and people don't come in a minute sooner and don't stay a minute longer than they are needed in our life.*

Surrender to the larger intelligence of the universe, to the reality of this moment, even if you don't like what you are seeing right now, for the Universe is guiding you to a better outcome. *When a lot of disappointments and lessons show up at once, it's not because life is against you, it's because the energy is supportive for your healing.* It would much rather take you through it quickly, than drag it out over a long time.

When you feel overwhelmed, it is important you move out of your head and into your body. Dancing, walking, exercising, yoga, meditation, or even a massage can help you feel more connected with your body. Try to connect with others, a friend, a pet, instead of sinking deeper. Find a way to get grounded, by taking a walk in nature, meditating or disconnecting from any technology or social media, or even by looking at any one element of nature. These basic tools promote a sense of well-being, which will allow you to release your emotional reserves to deal with everything that is going on in your life.

A student once went to his meditation teacher and said, "My meditation is horrible! I feel so distracted, or my legs ache, or I'm constantly falling asleep. It's just horrible!"
"It will pass," the teacher said, matter-of-factly.

A week later, the student came back to his teacher. "My meditation is wonderful! I feel so aware, so peaceful, so alive! It's just wonderful!'
"This too will pass," the teacher replied matter-of-factly.

Sometimes when we are really depressed, it helps to remember this basic lesson of life—stay equanimous under both the good and bad circumstances in our life, as nothing lasts forever.

We are all so good at amplifying what is wrong in our lives, what is disappointing, what is scary, what is unknown, what is holding us back. The negativity bias is very real as if paying attention to the threat is what keeps us alive, that we forget to focus on what is good. We forget all the joy, the ease, the grace, the comforts, the love, the support, the blessings that exist, because we take them for granted, and don't value them until we fear losing one of our blessings. Sometimes, we don't want to fully embody or experience what feels good, because we fear what will happen if it goes away. As if by not acknowledging its presence completely or overtly, we can avoid the hurt or disappointment if we were to ever lose it.

Hold on to the moments of happiness a little more, the daily small miracles, the tiniest of things we take for granted and amplify those in your mind. Be intentional and consistent about it and you will feel the grip of depression loosening its hold on you.

Wake up from this 'dream', become more aware, become conscious of the truth, of the purity of your soul. A 'woke' person acts with awareness and mindfulness and is considered 'awake' because they are aware of the truth of all existence. They are conscious of the truth that we are all divine souls enjoying a human experience and they take these setbacks in their stride. Every human being yearns for true, abiding happiness and peace—which can be found in the Self, the formless, indescribable perfection that is our infinite, eternal, being-consciousness.

In a world which makes it easy to live in a constant state of worry, choosing to live in the present is revolutionary. In a world that makes it easy to live in pain and suffering, choosing to live with joy is revolutionary.

Clearing Statements to Heal Depression:

Repeat 3 times each

For as many days as you need to say it:

- *I release my insecurities, fears, and doubts.*

- *I release my victim consciousness.*

- *I release my constant need for control.*

- *I release my anxiety over the uncertain nature of things.*

- *I release drama and conflicts from my life.*

- *I release the need to compare myself to others.*

- *I release all grief and trapped emotions that make me sad.*

- *I release all guilt for my past mistakes and actions.*

- *I release the demand for things to go exactly the way I want them to.*

- *I release all the patterns that keep me stuck in the same situations.*

- *I release all trapped energy, emotions and memories that make me restless and anxious.*

- *I release all blocks to love. I allow myself to receive and express love fearlessly.*

Positive Affirmations:

Repeat 3 times each

For as many days as you need to say it:

- *I deserve to be happy.*

- *I choose to be happy*

- *Life is an amazing gift.*

- *I am grateful just to be alive*

- *I attract miracles into my life*

- *Everything always works out for me*

- *My future is bright; filled with happiness and peace*

- *I revert to the present moment and restore my natural sense of flow*

- *I clear, balance, and energize all my chakras*

Walk the Path of Acceptance

Accepting reality, for what it is, is our first step to freedom from depression or anxiety. Stop insisting that things must go your way, on your timeline. No one is saying don't work to come out of that situation or change the situation, but denying its existence or fighting reality will only increase your suffering.

The first step to any change is accepting *what is.*

Anything that causes you extreme joy will carry with it the other polarity of causing you extreme pain when it ceases to exist. To stay equanimous under both circumstances is the only way to avoid your suffering when it ends. Nothing that is truly meant for you requires a tight grasp. The tighter you grasp when you have it, the higher is your suffering when it ceases to exist in your life.

If we can just remember that all things and people are temporary, and drop the illusion of permanence, we can save ourselves a lot of grief and heartache. Reality is always perfect just the way it is. Even if someone leaves you, or you lose a job, or have a falling out with a friend, know that it happened for your greatest good. We can never see the full picture at that time, but if we look back on our life, we know that sometimes things are not falling apart, they are simply falling into place.

We are never afraid of the unknown, we are afraid of the known coming to an end.

Acceptance is the letting go of the emotional resistance to the way things and people are. When you resist reality, you give the power of your emotional well-being to that reality, to other people, or events. You are basically saying that for you to be happy or at peace, others must act in a particular way at a particular time, and give you what you want, otherwise you have the right to be upset. Does that sound reasonable to you?

Acceptance helps to release the resistance and angst behind the situation. This allows you to channel your energies to find a solution to the situation at hand. We are not looking for a 'whatever' attitude of resignation, but to be genuinely accepting from the depths of our being. By choosing to remain open-minded and accepting of others, we give ourselves the opportunity to learn from others and affirm the interconnectedness we share. Those around us find more space to grow when we don't judge them by their past and we choose to perceive the good that exists in them now.

A better future is the result of creating a better present and improving our relationship with this moment exactly as it is.

As Byron Katie says, *"When you argue with reality, you lose, but only, 100% of the time".* Pain, loss, and injustice are inevitable. To accept them is not to sit back helplessly. Acceptance frees you to use your energy wisely, rather than deplete it with an unhealthy attitude that only adds to your pain. It is always good to do what you can to ease pain, comfort the grieving, and meet challenges, but first, walk the Path of Acceptance that is open in front of you.

When we make peace with the moment as it is and invest our

energy in creating the new, instead of resisting the present and the past, we are choosing to align ourselves with the most profound and lasting changes.

Accept what is. Accept what is. Accept what is.

Divine Instinct

Since the first man looked up in awe at the stars,
a profound instinct has existed in the human race.
This is the instinct which bids man look up,
which grants him the gift of hope and sustains him when life has
darkened,
which gives him courage even when all seems lost.

As an unfathomable and ever-present yearning,
this instinct to discover the Divine has never faded from the human
soul.
Since the dawn of Time,
this instinct has persisted in its belief
that the essence of life is good and joyful and true.

If you would live anchored in unshakable peace
and die with fearless dignity,
look deep into yourself and discover
that this instinct burns ever-bright within you.

Look deeper still and you will know
that the source of this instinct
is the immortal divine Self
That is your True Being

All suffering ceases—peace reigns supreme.
Here there is only perfect love and bliss.
The ultimate flowering of human consciousness
is to be the Divine that always is.

X

DISSOLVING OUR ILLUSIONS

Your inner freedom is of foremost importance. Then your outer world will follow. Your outer life is just a reflection of your inner state. The more peace you feel inside, the more harmony you will have in your relationships. When you have peace and joy on the inside, everything outside falls into place automatically. We allow all things, big or small, to steal our inner joy and freedom—such as struggle, guilt, expectations, complaining, and taking things more seriously than we need to. These emotions continue to attract undesirable experiences and emotions into our life, so the key to our happiness lies in releasing these low vibration thoughts. You cannot change or control people or circumstances around you, but changing how you think about and interpret them will make all the difference between peace and suffering in your life. No amount of guilt, resentment, or thinking can change the past. It is by fully accepting the present as it is, and where you are now, that you give yourself permission to move forward. *True freedom doesn't mean the absence of negative thoughts or emotions, but being free from your reaction to them.*

This is why the book, *A Course in Miracles*, says everything is an illusion, because we see everything from the polluted eyes of the ego with all its desires, complaints, and demands of how things should be. We can look at all these temporary things in life to fulfil us, but, at the end of the day, any real fulfillment can only come from our connection with Source. We are not connecting with Source often enough, and our soul laments that lack of connection with Source Energy. Any real fulfillment can only come from that connection.

The Illusion of Missing Out

In today's day and age, we are wired to keep going on and on, do multiple things to feel like we've accomplished something. We all have multiple hobbies, have multiple social invitations, travel plans, movies to see, friends to meet, goals to achieve that we have forgotten the Joy of Missing Out, the Joy of Simplicity. People feel depressed when they see other people's life on social media because it immediately evokes comparison in their mind. Thoughts like "I'm not as pretty as her", "We don't travel like they do", "They have so many friends", "I wish I was that close to my family", "Why am I still single?", etc. get evoked because of this comparison.

All of these things—whether it is excessive dependence on social media, or online content platforms—are an avoidance strategy to not see the sense of lack or emptiness we feel inside of us. A lot of human beings, at their core, feel empty. So they fill every waking minute up with work, TV, calls—just anything that makes them avoid feeling this void. We don't want to feel bored, lonely, sad, or frustrated, so we turn to these distractions to fill our inner sense of lack.

Freeing yourself up from unending commitments and online

addictions means more space and time for spontaneity, unplanned moments, and the surprise of chance encounters. For more of life to happen to you!

Your soul wants you to be free of this constant mental chatter. To be here and now in the present moment and enjoy the simplest things in life. To experience life at its purest essence.

Can you feel whole, complete, and content without any of these distractions? What will you do if you have no social plans? Can you spend time alone and be happy? Can you travel alone and be happy? *The ability to spend time with yourself and be truly content in that space is the sign of a self-sufficient and secure person.* These rare people are not looking for anyone to fill any void or emptiness or sense of lack in their life, they feel whole by themselves. They might enjoy the company of others and might want to have a loving relationship, but they don't need others to be happy. We must strive to reach such a place of completeness in ourselves. The more we enjoy our time alone, the more we expand our capacity to love and rejuvenate ourselves, and, in turn, enjoy our time with others as well.

Can you delight in the *Joy of Missing Out*?

Turn inwards, not outwards for a sense of fulfillment. This life is a precious gift. Every human being is born with a spiritual treasure—our integral divinity at the core of being. Discovering this spark and this stillness inside oneself, at the very center of one's own being, is the key to our inner freedom.

This stillness is the true source of your life force: omnipotent, infinite, eternal, and blissful.

The Illusion of the Ego

All Ego is Becoming. Becoming this or that. Becoming rich. Becoming fit. Becoming famous, becoming thin, becoming a people pleaser, finding a partner who can fill your void, receiving approval or appreciation. It does not let you stay at peace with what is, or without reaching these preconceived notions of what a perfect life looks like.

When one milestone is reached, the ego is already worrying about the next one, it can never be satiated, and if we are unable to meet all the checks on its list, depression follows. Ego misleads you to choose the wrong metrics of happiness that undermine your peace of mind. No one is asking you to not strive for success or to find love. But, not reaching these goals should not undermine your self-worth, and your happiness should not depend on it.

If you feel like a failure, it is because you are attached to judgment, and that judgment is coming from outside of you. You are defining who you are and where you should be in life, from the eyes of other people, rather than relying on your own ability to make decisions and regulate yourself.

It is important to move past self-stigmatization and have an authentic relationship with yourself. Calm your mind. You are on no one's journey, but your own. Pace yourself and live your life the way you want to. Don't let someone else's idea of success make you feel like you've chosen the wrong path.

Your inner state dictates your outer life, not the other way around. Most people have this backwards by making things outside of them more important, than what is going on inside them. What have you made more important than your connection with Consciousness, than your peace of mind, than your spiritual growth? What have you made into an 'idol' in your life, which you have begun to worship? *Idol worship*, in this context, alludes to the thing that you have made most important in your life—not a physical statue used in some religious practices. If money is more important than your connection with yourself or the divine, then money has become your idol; if some relationship is more important than yourself or your connection with the divine, then that relationship has become your idol. Fame, success, sex, the perfect body—whatever you have made as the most important thing in your life—becomes your object for 'idol worship'. You are idolizing these things more than your connection with your highest self. Do you want to continue to live this way?

Your ego is constantly planting a belief that you need something all the time—more money, more fame, more friends. No matter how many times you hear this truth—that none of these things matter, that none of these things are really needed to attain true joy—you refuse to internalize it.

If you really want to know what matters in the end, take advice from the dying. We regret the deeper stuff—not living our personal truths, not appreciating our relationships, not spending more time with friends, and not being honest about who we really are. How about making these the new metrics for your happiness?

- Personal growth and reflection time
- Degree of peace and harmony in your relationships
- Quality time spent with family and loved ones
- Taking the higher road when triggered
- Getting your self-worth from yourself
- Forgiving people from your heart
- Laughing a lot and making others laugh
- Offering random acts of kindness
- Making someone feel better about themselves today
- Offering genuine compliments to people around you
- Expressing gratitude to the Universe for everything that you already have

Once you start looking at and measuring your life from this new lens, you will deepen your connection to Source Energy, your journey into oneness with all of humanity, and with Consciousness.

The Illusion of Struggle

When we feel dissatisfied, the world outside becomes our enemy. We complain, blame others, and become a victim. The root of our suffering is attachment. When we can't let go, we create suffering. The things that were supposed to provide us happiness, now become our trap.

The illusion of suffering has misled us to believe that we must struggle to get what we want, that things don't flow to us easily. This is usually based on societal conditioning or conditioning by prior generations who taught us what they knew. We are deeply conditioned to believe that we must struggle to get what we want in life. Reality is, we don't have to. Yet, this simple reality is hidden from most of us in plain sight. So, we continue to do more and strive more, rather than stay in a state of Being that allows things to flow to us with ease and lightness.

When we are vibrating at the frequency of struggle and pain, we attract difficult situations that match our frequency. We all need to put in our hard work and the necessary efforts to achieve our goals, as that's how you tell the Universe what you want. However, the struggle and the excess hardship behind it all is quite unnecessary. We subconsciously attract this pain, this suffering, this struggle, this overwhelm, because we have conditioned ourselves to believe that unless we strive and push ourselves really hard, success will evade us.

This is a myth, a story we need to drop right away. Drop the story that suffering, stress, anxiety, and struggle are needed for us to survive and thrive. We put timelines and deadlines on things, so these limitations become our reality. We choose limiting experiences and attract situations and jobs that cause us to struggle to achieve our goals.

A martial arts student went to his teacher and said earnestly, "I am devoted to studying your martial system. How long will it take for me to master it?"

The teacher replied, "Ten years."
Impatiently, the student answered, "But I want to master it faster than that. I will work very hard. I will practice every day, ten or more hours a day if I have to. How long will it take then?"
The teacher thought for a moment, then said, "Twenty years."

Sometimes when we struggle and want something very badly, our energy and struggle pushes things away further.

We do not need to sacrifice our peace and joy in our pursuit of success or happiness. We have all accepted stress and struggle as a natural byproduct of life, these days. *That need not be so.* It is up to you to disrupt old constructs, transcend old ways of thinking, and create something fresh. In fact the less you do, the more you can be in *Being* energy than in *Doing* Energy, the more likely you are to achieve your goals and be in the flow of life.

Don't seek, don't search, don't demand, don't ask, don't knock.
Just relax. If you relax it comes, if you relax it is there, if you relax you start vibrating with it. –Osho

I have done Vipassana meditation twice in my life so far. In Vipassana meditation practices, we look deeply into the nature of suffering in order to clearly see the cause and effect relationship between resistance and suffering. This insight does not necessarily make the pain disappear, but the pain is experienced simply as it is—without the mind's reaction to it. Pain is, then, no longer feared or resisted. Like all phenomena, it is recognized as empty and impermanent.

Pain experienced without resistance is just another passing emotion.

Affirmations to Release Struggle

Repeat 5 times

Everything that is meant for me, flows to me easily.
Love, success, support, abundance, and good health all flow to me easily.
Miracles flow to me everyday.

All Will be Well

In a world going mad with fear and uncertainty,
have faith, stay calm, stay strong.
Do not give in to panic and despair; just do what you can each day to
help yourself and others.
Live fully in the present : alert, aware, conscious, anchored firmly in
Being.

Remember—everything will pass.
So every moment is a gift to be fully honored.
Use your time wisely to discover your divine nature that is your most
precious treasure.

An immortal, conscious, intelligent and omnipotent power is the
source and substance of all that exists.
You are one with that power.
Discover this in stillness, in silence, in the depths of your own being.

Once you experience this, there is no more fear or doubt—just perfect,
tranquil bliss.
Stay anchored in this state and let love and compassion radiate from
you like warm spring sunshine to bless and support all around you.
Whatever needs to happen will happen; what needs to be done will
be done.
All will be well.

XI

TRANSCENDING EXPECTATIONS & DISAPPOINTMENT

When we have expectations, we create a script of what a perfect life, a perfect relationship, a perfect friend should look like in our minds. Unknowingly, we assign dream roles to the people in our life to play that part, to respond to us in a certain way, to look a certain way, to do certain things and not do other things. Cultural or societal conditioning leads us to form these thoughts to fit everyone in a dream role. By doing this, we set everyone up for failure, and we set ourselves up for disappointment too. When people don't behave the way we want them to, we get hurt, angry or upset. We hold on to these thoughts about how everyone around us 'should' behave, and the stronger we hold on to these thoughts, the more rigid and difficult we become.

Who built this story, this script that this is how your partner, your family, your friends, or your coworkers should behave? *You* did. So that you could fill some void within you; so that you could stop feeling poorly about yourself. You keep fighting for specialness, love, and attention-all ego-driven desires. No amount of love and approval from someone else will change the way you feel about yourself. You hold on to these thoughts about how everyone around should behave, and the stronger you hold onto these thoughts, the more rigid and difficult you become.

Instead, what if you leveraged your relationships solely for your evolution? What if you used every hiccup, conflict, trigger, disappointment in your relationships to see what it reveals about you and resolve that knot inside you?

Who would you be without this conditioning, this story of how others are supposed to behave? Pure Love.

Expectations Fuel Misery

When you feel disappointed because you didn't get what you wanted, ask yourself why you needed that thing in the first place? Become very curious as to why you wanted it. What you'll begin to see is that the reason you wanted it, expected it, is because you want to know that 'you matter', to be seen, heard, appreciated, and acknowledged. This unmet need is what creates "lackness" inside of you, and you are using all the relationships around you only to complete this feeling of emptiness inside you.

Expectations or the need to control situations leads to misery because it is an expression of the lower self, fueled by fear and insecurity. Any form of entitlement from another is an attempt to get someone else to fill a void in you, to complete what's lacking in you. *This is a sure-shot path to misery.*

Every unmet expectation comes into our life to bring us into a deeper level of presence or a deeper level of resistance.

Once you drop your story of how others should behave, you allow yourself to experience them for who they are, not who you want them to be. Someone else's response or behavior has everything to do with *them* and what they are feeling and experiencing. It has *nothing* to do with you. Therefore, you must learn to not take it personally.

You cannot always transform others. You can, however, shift your perception and transform your state of being, and the direction it is taking. The difference between presence and resistance is connecting with your ability to accept people and situations the way they are and let go of the attachment of how things should be. This way you create space to be at ease in the present moment.

Tell yourself this:

People are doing the best they can today. This is all they have to give, and that is enough.

Expectation is a double-edged sword. It is just as tiring living up to other people's expectations of you. A life spent trying to please people or to do "what's expected of you," is a sure path to a regretful existence. Rather than being confined by other's opinions, you need to create your own reality. If you keep doing what others expect of you, you will lose your true joy for life. You will build resentment toward everyone else and get frustrated for not living out your own truth.

I believe that telling yourself not to have any expectations from anyone in your life is also creating an expectation from yourself to not have *any* expectations. This is a mysterious loop! It is an impossible and an unfair ask of yourself or others. It is neither realistic nor reasonable—to not have any expectations from anyone. It is perfectly ok to have reasonable expectations, as long as you don't allow those expectations to become a demand, as long as it doesn't turn into an entitlement, because *that's* what fuels your misery.

Deeper connections happen when the amount of love and support we give is not dependent on our expectations being met. When you drop all expectations of how someone else should respond or behave or act, you create mental and emotional space inside yourself to connect with them more freely.

Complaining Fuels Our Expectations

We are all so prone to complaining. We complain about everything multiple times a day—the weather, the people, the roads, the government, our company, our culture, our body, our weight—and we keep ourselves trapped in an endless cycle of negativity. This keeps us focused on what's lacking in our life, thereby attracting more of that into our life. *Complaining keeps us trapped in a vibration of self-pity and unmet expectations, both of which are highly disempowering thoughts depleting our vital energy.* What you are basically saying is that you cannot be happy unless everything goes according to the script you have written in your mind, for how this world should operate! Is that fair?

Voicing frustrations in small doses is ok, as it has its place as a stress reliever. However, most of us complain way more than our fair share and it becomes a bad habit. If you are a habitual complainer, you are essentially an 'energy vampire', as you deplete not just your own energy, but also the listener's energy field. You pollute not just your own mind, but also this beautiful planet with your negativity and lack of gratitude for what you have. You give up your own peace of mind when you insist that life and things and people should be a certain way. And if they don't, what do you do? Throw a tantrum by complaining?

We complain so much about our partners, without realizing that our partners are our greatest mirrors. It is a very toxic habit to keep complaining about them and trying to get them to change. People change when they are ready. Forcing someone to change leads to more conflict or guilt within themselves. Accepting and loving others as they are now, gives them room to do the same and to create space for a change. Every time we complain about someone, we are not accepting them for who they are. We are constantly rejecting them and telling them they are not enough. How do *you* feel when that is done to you? When you are asked to change, over and over again? When you are handed over a list of everything that's wrong with you? Chances are you don't like it one bit. Why, then, would others like to be at the receiving end of our complaining? *Do unto others what you wish them to do unto you.* Show your partner, your family, and your friends that you love them exactly as they are, in their entirety. It is the greatest gift you can give to anyone in this world.

Sometimes in extreme situations, it is important to walk away from a relationship that isn't serving you anymore, instead of continuing to stay in a perpetual state of disappointment. Either fix your expectations and accept the person and the relationship as it is or leave. Staying in a relationship and constantly complaining and being disappointed is no way to live. If you're worried that you don't have the strength to move on, think about how much strength you are using to hold on. Release all your old patterns before you move on to a new one, otherwise you will attract the same situations and circumstances in your next relationship as well. We repeat what we don't repair.

You might think that you are grateful for what you have, yet you complain about several aspects of your life. You cannot have a foot in each boat—decide if you want to float in the boat of gratitude or in the boat of complaints. If you are truly grateful for your life, then you have to embody gratitude everyday as a way of being, through all your interactions.

Have you ever wondered what it would be like to go without complaining for a week or a month? Look at the sky, look at the stars, look at the moon, *you are spinning in the middle of nowhere.* Comprehend the magic of it all, instead of being worried about the insignificant things that you complain about.

Transcending Disappointment

Every human being on the planet has an intrinsically deep relationship with disappointment. Not only have we been carrying it over lifetimes within us, we have even been projecting that disappointment onto all our relationships, and then, choosing to feel let down. It is so deeply rooted in our subconscious mind, that we don't even realize that we are seeking disappointment in our current life and continuing to project it on to others.

We feel disappointed and empty inside us, but instead of being aware of that, we look for someone or something around us to project that disappointment on.

What this means is that people are not choosing to disappoint us, as much as we are choosing the people who will disappoint us. Let that sink in. You are responsible for subconsciously creating situations to attract disappointment within those relationships in your life. You are only experiencing disappointment because you are choosing to experience it.

You will seek disappointment in a million ways, big and small, if that's what you are choosing to experience. If you are looking for disappointment, your lover will disappoint you, your family will disappoint you, your friends will disappoint you. You will unknowingly create situations and experiences where you will be disappointed. We remain so focused on our disappointment, that we fail to notice that even though people might be disappointing us on one count, they are probably surpassing our expectations on other counts, which we may not even be noticing, which we are taking for granted.

When you don't feel good, then you will create circumstances around you that will make you feel worse so that you can blame that situation or person for your unhappiness. There is a distinct possibility, however, that you were probably *already* feeling unhappy and disappointed from within, and that situation becomes an excuse to showcase your disappointment to the world. You create situations to deepen that feeling of disappointment and increase the turmoil in your mind and heart.

Sometimes you hold on to disappointment with a tight grip because it allows you to hold on to other disempowering emotions—for example self-pity, sadness, anger—which are also very addictive emotions. Before you know it, you spiral down quickly as one negative thought leads to another, and you're caught in an expectation-disappointment-blame game forever.

We keep playing this game of innocence and guilt, when in reality no one is fully innocent, and no one is completely guilty. We all take turns to play these roles.

Our souls carry this disappointment across lifetimes, which is our existential disappointment caused by our lack of connection with Consciousness, with Source. Our soul knows that any lasting joy and fulfillment can only come from this connection with the Divine. Our lack of connection with the Divine leads to existential depression. This is more pronounced in some and less in others, but we all carry it, whether we are conscious of it or not. The more evolved you are, the more sensitive you will be to these emotions.

When you are ready to heal disappointment in yourself, life will put you in situations where you will face a lot of disappointment from multiple people around you. You will be born in a family that will disappoint you, you will be surrounded by partners and friends who will disappoint you, because you are to use this life to transcend disappointment and not let it keep you trapped in an endless loop of despair. It is up to you to grab this opportunity, to realize that *all disappointment is our own projection.*

As a seeker, you know that when an emotion comes up consistently in your life, such as disappointment or anger, it needs healing and your opportunity to transcend it has arrived.

I have had two serious relationships, with the same pattern of disappointment in both relationships. The relationships would start off beautifully and then a year or two into the relationship I would start feeling disappointed in them on one count or another. There were three main reasons for this.

- Firstly, I grew up watching my mother express her disappointment in my father in many ways, despite the fact that she loved him dearly. It was just a compulsive habit. That habit became ingrained in my subconscious mind as a way of connecting in my relationships.

- Secondly, I subconsciously chose, and attracted, partners who would disappoint me. For example, if I was looking for romance and connection, I would end up choosing someone who wasn't very romantic. So how could I blame them for being themselves, for disappointing me?

- Lastly, I was projecting my soul's existential disappointment on to them, which is a universal issue, as explained earlier, with most of us on this planet.

The compounded effect of these three things caused disappointment to be a big theme in all my relationships. I was the writer, actor, director, and producer of this play called '*Disappointment*' in my life.

The day this was brought to my attention by my spiritual coach, I released all the disappointment I had been carrying, not just toward my partner, but toward all relationships in my life. It dissolved into nothingness in one miraculous instant. A huge weight was lifted off my shoulders. It transformed the way I began to relate to the whole world. From that moment on, I began to enjoy the people around me purely for their gifts and strengths and released all that inner turmoil of expectation and disappointment.

How can *you* do this?

Start to look at disappointment more objectively, in a detached manner from a distance, as just another passing emotion, a moment that *can* pass without stealing your peace of mind and happiness. The moment disappointment arises, just sit with it. It's just an emotion, a feeling, a thought, and this too shall pass.

Blundering Through

I made many mistakes in my life.
I was often unconscious and unaware.
This is the greatest and only sin, the root of all mistakes.
My learning took a long time.
Somehow, by the gift of grace, I blundered through into the Light.
So now, none of it matters.
I see with new eyes and a heart filled with gratitude.
I see that I never truly lost my real nature, the truth I was born with.
I see that the universe took care of me like a benevolent and tolerant
mother, no matter what I did.
I see that life is beautiful and sacred.
I feel the power of its mystery pulsing in my belly and my heart
And in the clouds, the trees, the light, the wind.
My spirit sings in harmony: it's so easy now-
All I have to do is tune in, and celebrate, and laugh
And live fully and totally in each magical moment of my life!

XII
ADVOCATING FOR YOUR OWN HAPPINESS

You are advocates of being as happy as you can be. Happiness is the act of finding joy in everyday experiences with other people. Happiness cannot be traveled to, owned, earned, worn, or consumed. Happiness is the spiritual experience of living every minute with love, grace, and gratitude. *You have to champion the cause for your own happiness, rather than expect it as a generous gift or donation from someone else.*

Happiness is a choice. That's right, *a choice*. Not an accident. Not a charitable gift from the universe. *A choice.* Of course, it's nice to fulfil your desires, and easy to be happy when you do. But happiness is about choosing to see the adventure in every moment, choosing to understand that there will always be light after the dark, that there is always good in every situation and every person, no matter how grim things may seem.

That's the key to happiness: choosing it. It's not an easy choice all the time, and it very well may be the last thing you want to do sometimes. When grief strikes, or when you just can't seem to catch a break, sometimes you just want to sulk and stay upset, and perpetuate the sadness. It is a natural response, but it isn't a required behavior, *it's a choice.*

Your happiness is your sole responsibility. No other person—or thing—can make you happy.

When you make other people responsible for your happiness, what you are really saying to the person is, "I feel this void or an emptiness inside me, which can only be fulfilled when you come and fill that void for me."

Is that fair? To you or that person?

When you avoid filling this emptiness with your own love, approval, attention, and joy, you shift the onus onto someone else and remain at their mercy, until you are ready to take responsibility for your own happiness.

All other so-called sources of happiness will only give you relative or conditional happiness, which is temporary, ephemeral, and at the mercy of meeting the endless needs of the ego. True joy, or absolute happiness, is a state of being in which you are filled with gratitude *all the time* irrespective of the state or stage of your life. You are happy just to be alive and don't need a person or a milestone to make you feel whole. This state of joy comes when you are deeply rooted in yourself. It is about returning to yourself and settling peacefully into the truth of who you are—not incomplete, not broken—*whole, lovable, and human.*

A happier, calmer person spreads more peace and joy around, so if you are ok, everyone around you will be ok too. Choosing to be happy will make you a better, stronger, wiser person. Fill your heart with self-love and you will become a magnet to attract more blessings into your life. Even if you don't have a reason to be happy, make it up, fantasize it. Decide you are going to be happy one way or another, no matter what happens. If you never have to work again, if you never have to watch TV again, if you never have to see that person again, you are going to be happy. Your happiness will not be at anyone else's mercy. You are going to be happy, no matter what.

Your main endeavor on this planet is to be responsible for your own happiness, to avoid polluting this world with any negativity, complain, blame, unhappiness, or projections.

Gratitude, Not Gratification!

Our ego keeps us trapped into believing that there are many conditions to be met to be happy. When one condition is met, we do feel a temporary state of "happiness". Then it is only a matter of time before we get restless and need to achieve a new milestone to feel happy again. The ego will create more conditions for you to be happy and will keep you going on this wild goose chase. In this chase, your happiness becomes dependent on some milestone or the other. Most of the activities we perform in our lives are useless because they are based on conditioning, conformity, and hypnosis of the world. From a normal person's perspective, playing this game of life is highly valuable. For a seeker who is looking for something more significant, something larger, all of these activities will seem pointless.

Real fulfilment and peace are present for each one of us right here, right now. There are no conditions to be met. Trust that your true happiness lies within you. Fulfillment is available within you, and is not dependent on external factors like money, success, relationships. Deep fulfillment is a part of you already, there is no chase needed. The poet, Kabir, calls it the *diamond in the pocket.* Which means despite being rich you look outside of you, like a beggar, for fulfillment. Once you focus inwards on this nourishing, fulfilling diamond, you will stop clinging to things available externally, in the world. If you live in a state of awareness about your Oneness with the Divine, you will not be desperate for anything.

Live your Truth; don't do only what's expected of you. You don't have to meet any expectations to be worthy of your own love and acceptance. Show up for yourself. Take the time to prioritize things that make you feel lighthearted and bring you peace. Show yourself some love. Be grateful and content with what you have. If you look around, you will find that you already have multiple reasons to be happy—there are so many blessings you have received in your life. Because we are so busy looking for the next best thing to fulfil our needs, we don't recognize happiness even when it is staring us in the face. One way to do this is to start writing down *all* the things that you have in your life that you are grateful for. When you make life about gratitude, and not gratification, you free yourself.

Stop looking for happiness in the wrong places. Stop fighting the wrong battles. Everything outside of you that you think brings you happiness, brings with it the duality of pain with it, when it ceases to exist. If that person or situation stops meeting your expectations or is taken away from you, you *will* feel pain. If that person now stands against you in *any* way, you will feel pain. Of what use is such fleeting happiness?

When do you become a true, spiritual seeker? When you have only one focus—deepening your connection with Source. As a seeker, you are being asked to see the futility of these worldly activities with awareness, that's all. You are not being asked to walk away from anything. Just observe your activities with detachment—whether you are striving for money, success, or fame to fulfil the demands of the ego. You must keep breaking through old structures, and flow beyond the boundaries of the ego, which is a very fragile structure, prone to fear. People will offer many justifications why you must keep running after something, they will not allow you to just be, to slow down, to accept long periods of downtime without guilt. They will cause you to keep running behind one thing or another, until you choose to break this cycle with conscious awareness and live your own truth.

The path to freedom is through detachment from your old habits of the ego. This constant whirling of the ego needs to be stopped, for you to feel true stillness inside. Then, your awareness will rise from this place of stillness and speak to you. When you let this awareness speak to you, you become a true seeker.

The Universe only wants to see us happy and grateful for receiving this gift of life, our wonderful planet and all its blessings, and all the experiences we are going through during our limited time on this planet. So, if you want to be happy, be!

Holding Your Thoughts Lightly

When you feel a surge of a negativity or any unhealthy emotion, you can observe it. Sit with it, witness it, and watch it come and go. Instead of resisting it or denying the negative emotion in any way, bring it into your loving awareness. When this happens, you will be able to step into another plane of reality which is the most elusive part of you—your soul. The soul, which notices and allows these emotions to exist with a quality of equanimity. Emotions can then come and go, without you getting caught up in a loop of reactivity. Accepting your negative emotions is akin to accepting your humanity. Allowing and accepting your humanity is the first step to happiness. Transforming it is next.

Transforming your thoughts about your life is not easy. But once you have learnt to build this muscle inside you, you move with surer footing toward liberation. Just like you don't allow thieves to enter your house and steal your wealth, do not allow negative thoughts to enter your mind and steal your happiness. It is never the person or situation around us causing us any grief or sadness, it is merely the interpretation of those events, which makes us miserable or happy.

When we hold onto our beliefs and opinions tightly, we are only indulging our illusions and exaggerations further, in the desire that it gives us personal identity.

Try it. Hold all your thoughts lightly in your mind and see how easy you feel. For example, if you feel, "my business partner is a fraud, he stole my money.", or "My boss drives me up the wall.", or if you hold strong opinions about your family, friends, or even the government, try saying, "*So what?*" Repeat it a few times, and you will feel that it leaves room for you to be flexible and feel lighter about that thought or opinion. Have you heard of the phrase 'Strong Opinions, Loosely Held'? Just like that. This simple technique allows you to free up your emotional energies and open your mind to other possibilities and perspectives.

Lightheartedness is key. Every time you are intense, angry, or emotional, ask yourself "*So what?*" or "*What's the worst that could happen?*" Then watch the thought lose its grip on you. Sometimes we assume that the worst will happen, which it rarely does, but even if it does, so what? You will deal with it and move on. By questioning the worst that could happen, you make your impending fears seem unreasonable and your anxiety reduces immediately. Try this "so-what" technique on as many issues in your life and lighten up your world.

It might seem overly simplistic, but it is highly effective in dramatically reducing the intensity of that thought in your mind. Make lightheartedness a regular coping technique. This is essentially a learned habit, and you can do it! As you build on the habit, it will get you through difficult periods. Laugh at the intensity of your own thoughts and tell yourself how ludicrous it is to be any other way.

Remind yourself often that nothing—that could happen either way—has any cosmic importance, it is all just a dream.

Doesn't this happen to you that in the middle of an intense situation, someone cracks a joke and everyone lightens up, including you? Suddenly you feel that you can actually process things much more easily and work toward a solution faster in this lighthearted state. So then, why not make this lighthearted state your new normal? Smile often, laugh often, or watch some comedy as part of your routine self-care package to see the lighter side of life.

A smile has the same effect. A smile, even if you are faking it, tells your nerves and your mind that everything is ok. That quickly breaks the chain of negative thoughts in your brain. Smiling can trick your brain into happiness. This has been proven by scientific research, as it reduces your cortisol, which is a stress-induced hormone. When you smile, dopamine, endorphins, and serotonin are released, which relax your mind. *Research has shown that there is a strong connection between your facial expressions and your underlying mental stress.* So, when you're feeling stressed, try forcing a smile on your face—research shows that this fake-it-till-you-make-it methodology might actually make you feel better!

Remember, lightheartedness is spiritual, a wiser path to enlightenment, peace and mental balance. It may be more effective than immersion at times when it comes to managing our stressors. In fact, lightheartedness is a key step toward being spiritual.

We didn't come here just to make it through life, we came here to thrive, to be happy, to enjoy all the blessings around us, to manifest miracles, to attract abundance, to spread joy, love, and laughter.

The Way to Paradise

Did you remember to Be today?
Did you experience the now, true presence in being—or were you lost in past and future, in fantasies and dreams and fears and desires?
Did you live today?
Or did the ticker-tape mind keep running non-stop so that you just stumbled unconsciously through the day?
Does the bird struggle with intellectual exercises to fly?
Does the fish need complex mental projections to plot its path in the ocean or does it just swim, without any doubts?
Why is it so difficult for human beings to just live naturally?
Because the human mind runs amok: out of control, twisting and churning in unnecessary agonies of thought, garbage spewing non-stop.
Can you turn it off? Can you use the mind wisely and only when required?
Can you stay in the thought-free state of pure being?
The way to Paradise is within you
in the stillness of your being, in the perfect grandeur of that Silence.

TRANSCENDING
OUR FEARS

A *Course in Miracles* tells us that there are no neutral thoughts, there are either fear-based or love-based thoughts. Every time your mind generates a thought, ask yourself whether this thought is based in love or fear.

Fear-based thoughts have a paralyzing effect on the whole organism, mind, body, and soul, as we get gripped with anxiety. We then engage in conduct that brings harm to others such as trying to control, to limit, to oppress, and to hurt others based on a need to control people and situations in our life.

How long will your fears continue to run your life?

Transcending our fears is key to facilitating a shift in our consciousness by realizing that we are our own power source, and channel this energy to help elevate the vibration of our thoughts and the intention behind our actions.

Trying to unlearn patterns of fear—inherited from our parents from the womb stage, through the different stages of growth, from infancy all the way into our adult conditioning—takes time. The "we need fear" school of thought assumes that we need societal precepts to keep us within the boundaries of acceptable behavior. You come alone into this world, you go alone, and while you are here, create and enjoy the experiences *you* want.

Our biggest fear is being seen for who we are, with all our vulnerabilities, our insecurities, our failures, our pettiness, our flaws, our anxieties, our humanness. So, we keep our masks on.

We should view our fears as our friends, not our enemies, because they reveal our deepest desires. Our fear of failure actually comes from a deep desire for success. Our fear of rejection or abandonment comes from a deep desire to be loved and accepted. Our fear of public speaking comes from a deep desire to be seen and heard. When we really want something, we fear putting ourselves out there to work toward it, because the fear of failing at your heart's deepest desire is even more painful. This stems from a lack of self-validation, self-confidence, and self-love. When you are filled with self-approval, you don't fear judgment or criticism from others. We prefer to deprive ourselves of that desire rather than face the fear of rejection. Our own self-limiting beliefs hold us back from achieving our truest potential and we learn to make peace with mediocrity.

Do you want to take a chance on yourself and expand, or do you want to keep playing life small?

What would you do if you weren't afraid of anything?

There is a lot of freedom when you transcend your fears and show up for yourself, whether you decide to start a business, join a dance class, take up theatre, try online dating, switch careers midlife, acknowledge your sexual preferences, move to a new city, or end a relationship. *You are powerful co-creators with this universe, and you choose and create every experience you have in your life.* You can face your fears by creating enough presence inside you, by becoming aware of what is happening, as well as your reaction to it.

Nothing Requires a Tight Grip

Sometimes you fear losing something really important to you because you get your sense of self from it, your job, your body, your beauty, your wealth, your relationship. What if that one thing you derive the most worth out of is taken away from you? Would you still feel whole and complete?

Sometimes you must lose what you place your worth in, so that you realize your worth doesn't live there.

Losing what you hold most dear to you—other than loss of life— can be the best thing to happen to you. You can either drown with that 'loss' or rise with it. You can choose to stay afloat as a human being in all your worthiness and wholeness or choose to lose yourself. You can choose to realize that you don't need anything outside of you to define who you are.

When I worked in the corporate sector, I derived my identity from my titles, awards, paycheck, and all the international work trips. So, letting go of my job and not being in control, initially, was frightening for me. A month into my sabbatical, however, I began to feel a huge sense of relief. Slowly, as my mental, emotional, and physical health returned to wholeness, I took great pride in my decision to walk away from what was not serving me anymore and for choosing to prioritize my wellbeing. I realized that my self-worth comes from *me*—and *not* my job or my startup. This was a huge milestone in my spiritual journey, as it would be for anyone who is freeing themselves from the prison of the ego, the mind, and the rat race. I became less interested in keeping up with external expectations and more interested in how my own expectations were serving me. Or not. That's where my growth, my freedom came from, and that's when I *finally* found myself.

One of the biggest, most universal fear is the fear of losing love or a loved one. And this fear keeps us trapped in interpersonal dynamics which are not healthy for us.

We all look for different things in our relationships. Some people value truth so much, that they're willing to feel immense discomfort in order to receive it. Some people value freedom so much, that they'll walk away from relationships that interrupt it. Some people value connection so much, that they'll give up their own dreams to maintain it. Our partners may not value the same things we do, and in many cases, coexistence becomes hard and the relationship becomes dysfunctional. It seems impossible to let go of this person, even though we feel highly unfulfilled. These relationships are not hard to let go of because of love. Love is free. You can never lose love in the truest sense because *love is who you are.* They are hard to let go of due to your attachments and fears.

What most of us embody are attachments, codependency, conditioning, addictions, fear of loneliness, and abandonment.

Codependency is the chronic neglect of self in order to gain approval, love, identity through another person. We learn these patterns or coping mechanisms in childhood and play out those patterns in our adult relationships. It hurts really bad to let go of some people, because you're not really letting go of the person, you're letting go of something within you that this person represented or triggered, and you're associating that emotion with this person physically.

A friend of mine was in a difficult marriage for a really long time, but the couple stayed together for the sake of their 5-year old child, and also to protect their image of a perfect family. She feared being alone, she feared her son would never be happy without both parents, she feared judgment from her family; and all these fears kept her trapped in a *prison of her own making*. The relationship gave her an identity, and she didn't want the mask of a perfect life and a perfect family to come off. And then one day, he left her and filed for divorce. She went through tremendous depression, self-pity, and stayed in victim mode for a really long time, blaming him for all her unhappiness.

A year into her therapy, she realized that her ex-husband was not the perpetrator and she was not the victim. He simply had the courage to walk away from something that was not serving him anymore. She found a new job and after a year she was in a loving relationship with someone she met at work. Dropping her fears lifted a big weight off her shoulders and here she was, on the other side of her fears, taking charge of her own happiness.

As the storm clears, and your fears fade away, you meet the next
version of yourself.

So, remember this when you're in the middle of a hard break up—you're being invited to let go of what doesn't serve you anymore. This is your opportunity to evolve, to empower yourself, and to release patterns that have been hindering you from receiving what you truly deserve.

A healing path often appears when everything else has been stripped away, when love is lost, when the promises are broken. It is in our moments of despair and in being shattered to smithereens, that we are being prepared for a more awakened existence.

Clearing statements to release the fear of losing love

Repeat 3 times each

For as many days as you need to say it:

- *I release the Fear of Losing Love.*
- *I release the Fear of Being Unloved.*
- *I release the Fear of Being Alone.*
- *I release the Fear of Starting Over.*
- *I release the Grief of Losing Love.*
- *I release the Grief of Being Unloved*

Unspoken expectations are silent relationship killers. To have a conscious relationship, you need to be courageous enough to be vulnerable in front of others.

Be vulnerable. Be authentic. There is a beauty in vulnerability. The more you open up as yourself, the more attractive you become. Vulnerability allows you to be truly authentic with another person by allowing yourself to be seen. What happens then is magical. *When you stand in your truth and let the other person witness who you are, it creates a bond that cannot be broken.*

What if we want to tell someone what we really think of them or express something unpleasant to them, but we fear how it will be received, and, hence, shrink ourselves or what we are saying, or tip-toe around them and spend more time managing or thinking of their reaction, instead of honoring what we want to express. When you don't trust their emotional regulation, there is a tendency for us to do some of on their behalf. Because we fear losing them, we continue to tolerate wrong behavior from them, just to avoid the boat from rocking. We play small because of someone else's inability to take feedback and regulate their emotions. So, what is the best way to handle this?

First, let's start by emotionally regulating *ourselves* and the space we are coming from before we express ourselves. *Then* we can invite others to do the same. We need to see why this fear is coming up for us and remove any need for control, manipulation, or judgment attached to what we want to express. Once we remove all fear, all emotion from it, then we can share our experience and feedback with this person more objectively. This is called Conscious Communication, based on the basic premise of mutual respect. If they still react back violently, then managing their emotional experience is not your job. That's their karma, let them deal with it.

Now flip the script here and ask yourself:

- Can others trust me with Conscious Communication?

- Do others have to think a lot before they can come to me? Am I open to feedback?

- Do they fear I will be angry or defensive, or maybe that I will shut them down?

- Is there a need for something to shift inside me, so that others can open up more freely in front of me?

Explore these questions and see what comes up for you.

Affirmations to clear Fear:

Tap along your EFT points, as you say these out loud for added healing

- *I am not afraid today. My fear is not real.*

- *I am brave enough to take chances. My fear is not real.*

- *I can handle anything that comes my way. My fear is not real.*

- *I choose to take a chance on myself. My fear is not real.*

- *Even if I fail, it will make me stronger. My fear is not real.*

- *My struggles are opportunities to grow. My fear is not real.*

- *I am capable of achieving my goals. My fear is not real.*

- *My abilities are limitless. My fear is not real.*

- *I will overcome all obstacles. My fear is not real.*

- *I have what it takes to conquer my fears. My fear is not real.*

Transcending Collective Fear

These days, it seems, we face a daily barrage of things to fear, at both a personal level, and collectively as humans. Whether it is an economic crisis, environmental collapse, diseases, terrorism, wars, natural disasters, or even a global contagion.

Stay grounded and steady in your choices as you release anyone or anything that no longer serves you. Create healthy energetic boundaries so that you are not sucked into the whirlwind of anger, fear, and negativity that may be swirling around you. Because you tune in energetically to your environment, be discerning about the people you spend time with, and the environments you inhabit. Consciously consider where you live, work, and spend most of your time.

Take a break from all kinds of media and the constant bombardment of bad news and images. Focus on the controllable elements in life, such as looking after yourself and your family, and taking necessary precautions. You serve everyone best when you are alright and happy and in a state of high vibration yourself. If you allow yourself to be carried away with collective anxiety and confusion and fears, then you serve no one.

To transcend this dark cloud of unenlightened, unconscious thinking, I invite you to become a drop in the vast ocean of love by taking responsibility for your choices, and to practice daily gratitude, compassion, and forgiveness. Focus your energies on the positive aspects of your life, and trust that you have the power to transcend any fear that blocks your evolution and growth.

Here is a small exercise to release the grip of any personal or collective fear:

Write down your fears, because when you name and acknowledge them, they lose their grip on you.
Once you write down your fears, say them out loud.
Then burn that piece of paper.

In many cultures and healing practices, fire is a powerful cleansing ritual. You feel significantly lighter and at ease after burning that paper. Try it.

Sinking

I shut my eyes, but my mind still spins visions of improbable worlds.
I stop up my ears, but my mind still echoes with endless sounds.
I close the door of all five senses: alas! still no peace to be found!
I give up in total surrender and sink like a stone into me.
Mind drowns in the Heart and dissolves
like a lump of salt in the sea.
Listen, my friend—die now before the body dies
And be free.

SELF-LOVE, DECONSTRUCTED

Self-love is being your authentic self and accepting and loving yourself exactly as you are with your strengths and shadows alike. It is the ultimate tribute to your highest self and your connection with the divine.

What does that mean? It means loving every part of you, *even the parts that are not so lovable.* It means accepting your strengths, your flaws, your victories, your failures, your mistakes—*all* of it.

Your relationship with others is a reflection of the relationship you have with yourself. When you love yourself unconditionally, you will love everyone around you unconditionally too. And if you can't love and accept yourself fully, you cannot truly love and accept anyone else either. So, healing your relationship with yourself first is the key to healing your relationship with others.

Know that *you are enough.* Breathe that thought deep into every part of your body. *You are enough* does not mean that you don't need help, or that you are self-sufficient in life, or that you are flawless. It only means you are enough as you are, mess and all, beautiful and broken, showing up for life every day. *You are enough means that you don't have to strive to become more worthy, more valid, more acceptable, or more loved.* You already are all of those things.

Let's deconstruct and understand all the key ingredients of Self-Love:

- Self-respect, self-appreciation, self-care, self-acceptance, and self-compassion.

Self-respect is the most critical element of self-love. It helps you to define your own worth and value as a human being. People respect those who respect themselves. Respect yourself for who you are, value your unique approach to life and place a premium on your own self-worth. If you have low self-respect you will engage in acts of self-rejection—like chasing people to be included or pretending to be someone you are not. You don't need to lower your standards to keep anyone. Learn to honour yourself before you honor anyone else.

There is something wrong if you are not the most important person in your life.

Self-appreciation is learning to appreciate the magic that you are. Any reluctance on your part to overtly appreciate yourself, is a sign that you don't think you are worthy of receiving that appreciation and praise. Hence, this becomes the very reason to do this. Appreciate yourself to activate your self-esteem and remind yourself about your strengths. Try this technique below, it is effective and often suggested by therapists as well:

- *Take a journal and write down all the qualities about yourself that you appreciate and like.*

- *Write down all the ways in which you make others happy, all your wonderful strengths, skills, qualities.*

- *If you can't think of many things, ask five of your closest friends to tell you what they like most about you.*

- *Do this at least once a year*

This seemingly self-indulgent act can be a powerful tool to activate your self-confidence and self-love.

Self-acceptance is accepting yourself completely—just the way you are—with your strengths and flaws alike. It doesn't mean you become complacent with your weaknesses. It means you stop punishing yourself for them. Learn to practice true accountability without punishing yourself. Which means accepting yourself completely with love and compassion, then work to release your flaws and evolve as a human being.

When we reject ourselves for our flaws, we reject everyone around us for theirs too. Most of us don't realize that if we keep rejecting the parts of us which we don't like, we land up projecting our rejection onto others, and, in turn, attract rejection too. Any judgment and rigidity toward another is a reflection of the judgment and rigidity we hold toward ourself. There are parts of us we resent, we hide, we are ashamed of. Those are the very parts that need the most amount of love, as they are all hiding behind some old, unhealed wounds.

Perhaps the missing piece in self-acceptance is accepting those parts of you that are not acceptable.

Perhaps this goes against your idea of perfectionism, but it is deeply relieving to know that you don't need to work tirelessly to accept each and every unacceptable part. That, in itself, is a deep level of self-acceptance.

Self-compassion entails being kind and understanding toward ourselves when we suffer, fail, or feel inadequate, rather than filling ourselves with self-criticism. Actively try to soften this harsh inner voice and to replace it with a kinder one. Self-compassion isn't about falling into complacency, with no intention of changing what isn't working for you. It's about accepting your full humanity in order to change what isn't working for you. It's about relating to yourself in a way that supports your transition. Self-compassion is not about talking to yourself like a Zen master. It's about talking to yourself in a way that you would talk to someone, who you see value and goodness in.

Try this exercise:

- *Close your Eyes. Imagine a miniature version of you in your heart who is criticizing you and shaming you for your flaws.*

- *Look at that part of you and fill it with a white light of love and compassion till that inner voice, coming from this miniature version of you, quietens.*

- *Once that mini-you is filled with light, you will instantly feel an inner stillness and silence in your heart.*

Allow yourself to be human, to fail, to make mistakes, to fail. And then to rise again. This is the dance of life.

Self-care helps you to feel nurtured and looked after, and it raises your vibration and frequency to attract even more blessings. Doing something just for yourself is an essential part of reclaiming your mental and emotional energy. As you set aside time for yourself, you notice that your motivation to be absorbed more fully in life and to be there for others increases as well. Rest and self-care are vital for your emotional, physical, and mental well-being. When you take time to replenish your spirit, you serve others from the overflow. You cannot serve from an empty vessel.

- *Write down a list of all the things you would like to do just for yourself. Maybe it's a weekly salt-water bath, maybe it's time in a spa. Maybe it's taking a meditation class, a dance class, a cooking class, journaling, blogging, hiking, or learning how to fly a plane. This list must include things beyond your hobbies—anything that brings you a place of nurture and self-care.*

As you meet, acknowledge, accept, forgive, love, and appreciate yourself on many different levels, you begin to experience the world as more positive, supportive, and loving. You awaken parts of yourself—that have been denied, ignored, or forgotten—in a gentle way. You bond with your inner child. You embrace your humanness and your divinity equally, as if they are no longer separate.

To love yourself *also* means to heal yourself, heal your wounds, heal your inner child. When you take the time out of your life to heal yourself, become more positive, more radiant with love and happiness, you are taking care not just of yourself but everyone who comes in touch with you in your world.

You are 'The One' You are Looking For

"The One" is not outside of you. You are it. You are "the one" you are looking for.

What if you never had to search for anyone ever? What if you just needed to find yourself!

What if you realized that the pot of gold that you are looking for at the end of the rainbow is YOU! How does that thought make you feel? Would that be a relief? Or would it be a fear-inducing thought? This can be a very scary thought for some, and, yet, a very freeing thought for others. Which one is it for you? Not everyone can learn to give up their codependency and lean just on themselves.

Your spiritual mission is not to find someone to complete you. It is to return to your innate wholeness.

You are your one true love. Many of us look for 'the right one', the 'love of our life', someone to 'complete us', so that we can feel loved or fulfilled. All such relationships, in the beginning, bring us so much happiness and excitement, such a sense of belonging and nurture. But as time passes, the same relationship becomes a source of feeling unhappy, trapped, or otherwise unfulfilled. When you expect other people to fill your hearts to make you feel whole and complete, you are basically entering these relationships from a place of scarcity and deficiency.

We don't look as much for anything outside of ourselves, as we do for love. We are constantly searching for reassurance that we are loved. We want to be seen, heard, and, above all things, loved. However, we also have an expectation of what that looks like. We have already defined how that love should be expressed by our parents, peers, friends, and our partners.

The trouble with that is that when we expect love to be expressed in a specific way, we overlook what love really is. We overlook the love that we are receiving and the way that we are receiving it currently. Allow love to flow freely into your life just the way it is, without all the grasping, clutching, clinging, begging, needing, and chasing.

I have no interest in grasping—only in allowing
I have no interest in being pedestaled—only in being seen
I have no interest in solving life—only in living it
I have no interest in proving—only in sharing
I have no interest in perfection—only in wholeness
—Lisa Olivera

Everything you're searching for is within you. Find that ecstasy within yourself. Validate your own existence as a human being. Validate your feelings and emotions and pay attention to your own needs. I'm sure you've heard this multiple times before, I'm still going to go out on a limb and say it again—*When you stop searching desperately for love, it will find you when you least expect it.*

Why exactly does this happen? When you like yourself, when you love yourself, you start vibrating at a higher plane. That self-confidence and self-love is what makes you so irresistible to others. When you come at life from a place of *being love* yourself, the Universe matches that vibration. When you start feeling whole in yourself and don't need another to complete you, that's when you attract the right person. If you feel broken and incomplete you will attract another broken and incomplete person. So, invest time and effort in becoming whole first, then you will not need to *seek* a partner—you will simply attract them.

Learning to choose yourself is hard.
Not choosing yourself is harder.

To be yourself, to choose yourself, also means to be your authentic self. To be authentic means to be in alignment with your true self. To accept yourself in all your humanness and connect from the real parts of who you actually are. Be genuine. Be real. Self-worth and self-trust allow you to show up as yourself. There is no right or wrong, there is just you.

Be Your Own Guide

We all seek gurus, teachers, mentors, therapists, and spiritual coaches to guide us on our path. These people serve like angels on our path to help us course correct, especially when many things in our life seem to be going off course. They help dig us out of the hole we put ourselves in. Spending time with such guides is a special treat you can give to yourself. This is one way you demonstrate self-love, not just by buying clothes, shoes, and other material experiences; but, also by investing in yourself through sessions with such guides.

However, a good guide will *always* empower you to ultimately rely on your own knowledge and instinct to guide yourself. A good guide will be with you till you start to trust your own instincts and use your inner compass to guide and direct your own future. True awareness is a permanent part of our being, like a pot of gold that you are sitting on all along. The best guides and teachers will redirect you to this pot of gold *inside* you and, over time, make you aware that you already possess all the intelligence, knowledge, and intuition that you are seeking outside. *That's* when you know you are working with the right guide, when they don't allow you to use them as a crutch forever.

Reaching that point where you can rely on yourself requires you to heal your triggers, projections, patterns, and shadows through some deep inner work first, which you have already begun to do through the course of this book.

Once you are on the path that is right for you, and have reached a certain level of self-awareness, knowledge, and understanding on your spiritual journey, you can very safely rely on yourself to be your own guide. You will be able to reach higher levels of evolution by using the world as your mirror and remembering all the lessons you have already learnt so far.

How do you know that you have reached a level where you can self-sustain? When you have more peace and harmony in relationships around you. When you don't care as much about proving yourself to others. When you consciously carve out time every day to look inwards, instead of filling every moment with work, social media, online TV, or nonstop social engagements as a way of avoiding your own emptiness. *When you're able to go within to get the answers, rather than having to wait for someone else to answer it for you. When you are able to find stillness in the chaos around you and meaning in seeming trivialities. That's when you know.*

You can get to this stillness via meditation. Meditating daily is a sign of depth and maturity, a way to connect with Source every day and bring some inner stillness and depth to your soul. In this calm state, you are able to raise your own vibration, enabling yourself to find the right answers to anything. You can trust your own judgment when you operate from this place of stillness. Once you have reached a level of inner stillness, peace and self-discipline, you can reduce your dependency on your mentors or guides, and you can finally become your own guide.

Our inner world has a magnetic force that draws to us what we need to evolve to the next level. We have everything that we need to move forward on our paths to self-realization. *So, when you are on your path, and sometimes don't know which way to turn, just turn in to yourself.* The answer may not come rationally or intellectually. But, if you simply ask a question in a state of stillness and wait for the answer, it will come to you. To cultivate this connection with your innermost voice, it is imperative that you meditate every day. It *will* allow you to trust your intuition completely, and soon your intuition will be the basis for all the decisions you make in your life. The more you practice this, the more you will trust yourself, the less you will look outside for guides, and you will, at one stage, become your own teacher.

Remember, these lessons of Self-love

- *You don't need to wait for someone to come in to save you. Save yourself.*

- *You don't need anyone to complete you. You are already whole.*

- *Choosing yourself means putting your own needs first. Make yourself a priority.*

- *Recognize what no longer serves you. Release it from your life.*

- *Acknowledge what you do well. Acknowledge your gifts.*

- *Let go of the need to prove yourself. To anyone.*

- *Allow yourself to be different. Be you.*

- *Learn to say no when you want to say no. Practice and live your boundaries.*

- *Do what is right for you, even when it is hard. Own your space.*

- *Remind yourself every day of how powerful you are. Live your power.*

- *You don't need anyone to choose you. Choose yourself.*

Because if you don't, you will always be at the mercy of someone else to make you feel good about yourself. That is no way to live.

You will run out of patience with yourself several times. You will tire of how you break and mend repeatedly, how you shift between self-acceptance and self-loathing, how you soften and harden, but through all of that, you deserve a lot of love. — Billy Chapata

Self-Love Affirmations:

Repeat 3 times

I am Divine, I am Transcendent,
I am Free, I am Love,
I am Magical, I am Creative,
I am Powerful, I am Consciousness,
I am Eternal, I am The One.

We cannot *find* love or *give* love, we can only *be love.* Conscious Love.

Conscious Love is when you have become a statement of love, and you are not trying to do anything to demonstrate your love to anyone, you are just *being love.* When you are being love, all you experience is a feeling of flow with *everyone* in the universe. You are in love with the universe itself. That's what this game is all about. You have to give up the blockages inside you that prevent you from Being Love. You must remember that the object of your love is love itself. When you live in love, you see love everywhere you look.

To reach this state, you could start by living your life in a conscious way, by being loving, warm, affectionate at all times as a way of being. This will get you home, closer to your awakening. Keep allowing your lives to become more and more simple, more and more harmonious.

Repeat 3 times:

I am loving awareness
I am loving awareness
I am loving awareness

Perfection

This is perfect. That is perfect.
I am perfect. You are perfect.
The land and the sea and the heavens are perfect.
The birds and the beasts and the insects are perfect.
Atoms and cells, stars and galaxies, clouds and trees, lives and deaths, rebirths and resurrections are all perfect.
Subtract the perfect from the perfect—only the perfect remains.
Divide the perfect by the perfect—only the perfect remains.
Create the perfect, transform the perfect, destroy the perfect—only the perfect remains.
Transform yourself! Be perfect.

THE ART OF GIVING AND RECEIVING

In life, we are constantly in a state of giving or receiving with others, and with our beautiful planet. Our basic act of breathing is also a combined act of taking and giving—we breathe in as much as we breathe out. We have reduced giving and taking down to a barter exchange of material things. In the truest sense, the act of giving and receiving expands to include time, love, knowledge, attention, support, loyalty, and so much more. There are a multitude of ways we give and receive. Spiritually, this concept of giving and receiving is intertwined in much deeper ways than we understand in the normal parlance of give and take.

The Art of True Giving

When we practice the art of giving, it is important that we give freely from our heart, with no expectations, and without holding back. Giving our best to others, without expecting to receive in return, simply means we are choosing to share the abundance we already have within us, and that more will continue to come to us, even if from another source. Only when we give from a place of love without demands, can we feel truly fulfilled and experience *authentic giving*. When we attach an expectation of what we should receive in return, we taint our giving and turn it into a mere transaction.

True authentic giving entails placing no demands on what others are to do in return, allowing us to keep giving from an overflow of abundance within us.

When we give from this pure place in our hearts, we are allowing love and abundance to flow freely. When we are not thinking about receiving in return, we are giving our best to support the happiness of those around us. Whenever we manage to give without expectations, calculations, negotiations, etc., we are indeed in heaven.

When you can give freely, because you know that there is infinite abundance in the Universe, *know* that you will *always* be abundant—no matter how much you give away.

You give but little when you give of your possessions. It is when you give of yourself that you truly give. — Kahlil Gibran

When we give without expecting, it creates a better world and releases the barriers to receive abundantly too. When we open our hearts to give from an abundant place, we will naturally and automatically receive in return. We always receive what we give. But, if we put desperate or needy energy into our actions, what we receive in return might be so because the other person feels compelled to return our favor, not because they truly *wish* to nurture us.

Conditional giving blocks our openness to receive. When we withhold our generosity from others, because of certain conditions or expectations, what we are doing is withholding generosity and love from flowing abundantly toward ourselves too. *Withholding our generosity is not a punishment to others as much as it is to ourselves.* Relationships grow when we give our best, despite what we are currently feeling, without letting temporary situations or emotions limit the amount of love we give. When we limit our giving, believing others *must do something* to be deserving of it first, we block love from flowing freely within ourselves too.

Downside of Over-Giving

When you go above and beyond for people on a regular basis, you run the risk of being taken for granted. You also get to hear, "I never asked you to" from them in return. When you over-give, you continue to settle for someone else not showing up.

While you can be a very loving person, you still can't help but create a scorecard of your giving and create unspoken expectations that are tied to your "unconditional love". By doing their work, their part in the relationship you feel that you are proving your love, but it also proves that you don't have your own back. You then sit on your self-righteous throne after doing all you can to hustle for love and wonder why the other person doesn't choose you, without realizing that you are not choosing yourself either. You are left empty and resentful toward them for neglecting you. What you don't realize is that you are the one who neglected yourself in the first place. A boundary is not only about what you allow in your life, but also how you show up for yourself, how you conserve love and energy for yourself too.

> **Allowing—and creating the space for—other people to do their part and show up for you, is important to maintain balance and equilibrium in our relationships.**

I have been a compulsive giver in my romantic relationships, where I have surprised my partner with gifts and experiences, and done a multitude of things to pamper him, to make him feel special, in the hope of receiving appreciation or attention in return. When he was unable to reciprocate, a silent frustration and disappointment built toward him. My ego would trick me into believing that I was giving without any expectations. But, if that were really true, I wouldn't feel this immense hurt when my efforts went unacknowledged. I also realized that I needed to get better at allowing myself to receive as well and make room for my partner to show up for me.

Give because you enjoy how it makes you feel about yourself, because you enjoy helping others, because seeing them happy in turn makes you happy, and for absolutely no other reason in the world. True giving is ultimately an act that makes us feel better about ourselves and makes the receiver of our giving feel good too.

Dark Side of Compulsive Giving

Have you ever been around a compulsive giver? Maybe *you* are one yourself!

When we observe a compulsive giver, we see them as an altruistic, empathic, and caring human being. In reality, in most cases, deep inside that compulsive giving comes from a need to please people and create a codependent dynamic.

If you are a compulsive giver, you will tempt and cajole people around to avail of your services, or money, and in some subtle way force your magnanimity on to others. It will make you feel like you are needed by others and, that, perhaps, others will be grateful or indebted to you; that perhaps, this sense of indebtedness will make them like you more. Welcome to the dark side of giving! Inevitably, this leads you to develop unrealistic expectations, as you feel that people should be immensely grateful to you and their gratitude should translate into some kind of fawning or obsequiousness. When, eventually, you face a lack of reciprocity, as you surely will, because no one can match your level of giving, you will judge everyone else for exploiting you and for being ungenerous. You will slowly start seething with anger, and, sometimes, even find yourself getting aggressive!

It is important to bust our myths about compulsive giving. It is *not* as altruistic as it seems, however it is not rooted in evil either. It is a complex phenomenon-the desire to do good along with the desire to feel important and needed, in order to establish control on the receiver.

Giving is often where we place power. We get a lot of credit for giving, and, so, when we give on a regular basis, we may run the risk of beginning to look at ourselves as more important than those we give to. A compulsive giver is unable to deny anyone's requests, even when these are not explicitly expressed, as a figment of their own neediness. They cherish and relish their self-conferred victimhood and nurture their grudges by maintaining a detailed account of *everything* they give and receive. A compulsive giver also creates blocks to receiving, as they hold the belief that people only want to take from them and, hence, they create blocks to receiving. They find it difficult to receive, mainly because accepting things from others would require them to drop the illusion, that they have to lookout for themselves and that no one else will take care of them. Thus, the lack of reciprocity just feeds a spiral of disappointment and pain for them.

The Art of Receiving without Guilt

We have all of this beautiful love to give. We just give it away, and we show up so effortlessly for others. But when it comes to allowing people to show up for us, a lot of us often struggle. Maybe we reject it, deny it, hide from it, or simply do everything ourselves, so there is no room for anyone else to step in. For example, being a great partner isn't just about what we do for our partners, it's also about what we allow them to do for us; what we do to create a space and a role for them, so they can feel they have a purpose in our lives as well. Great partnership goes both ways. You *have* to find ways to receive as well, you cannot just be a giver. That is not the *only* role chalked out for you.

Why is receiving hard for some of us? When we give, we are in control in a certain way. Receiving requires a higher amount of vulnerability than giving. Receiving invites us to welcome a vulnerable part of ourselves where we need to accept that we need support as well. Accepting our vulnerability makes us human, and we open a part of ourselves that feels real and almost childlike. If we can offer help to others when they need it, we should feel just as comfortable receiving support in times of need. That's how the Universe maintains balance, and that's how we maintain equilibrium in our life too. *If you cannot receive, then it is not ok for you to give either.* Our reluctance to freely receive affects our relationships with others and limits our openness to Grace. Getting better at receiving, then, should be a vital intention of our spiritual practice.

Consider the narratives that keep you stuck.

- What did receiving feel like and look like in your family?

- Were you allowed to have needs?

- What conversations about giving and receiving do you have (that may not even be yours)?

- What beliefs do you have about allowing others to take care of you or support you?

Many of us grew up believing that it is nobler to give, than to receive. Our religious beliefs or cultural constructs may have had us believe through our lives that it is selfish to receive. They may have even celebrated giving way more than receiving, that it is better to be self-effacing and not bring attention to ourselves. As a result of such conditioning we feel shame in receiving. These edicts prevent us from receiving all the blessings that could otherwise come our way quite easily.

We fail to understand that receiving creates connection. Prioritizing giving, over receiving, maybe a way to keep people distant and our hearts protected. To the extent that we fear intimacy, we may disallow ourselves from receiving anything—from a gift or a compliment to support and love—thereby depriving ourselves of a precious moment of connection. Take compliments and words of encouragement, gracefully. Resist any temptation to downplay or minimize positive things people say about you.

Make a practice of consciously acknowledging your vulnerability and dependence upon others. During a meal, choose one food item and try to list all the people who helped bring it to your table—the farmers, truckers, store managers, package makers, and even those who created the map that facilitated its movement from its place of origin to your table. Make a habit of acknowledging one free gift you have received at the end of each day. Then, thank the Universe for the bearer of the gift.

You receive when you open up fully to take in what is already coming your way. *All* the physical things that come from creation—including food, shelter, the beauty of nature, the warmth of your home. *All* the love that comes to you from other people, your whole human experience, all the love the Universe gives you—that melts your heart and nourishes your soul. Part of the process of receiving is cherishing what you are receiving.

Cherishing, even adoring, the source of the gift—whether it is a person, a circumstance, or the very source of life—nourishes our soul.

Returning Home

Thoughts and dreams and fantasies drifting by
Nothing to grab or hold onto, empty sky.
I fall like a stone into myself, so deep inside
Deep down, down into silence, nowhere to hide.
I hear the sound of emptiness like a distant bell
Where the Light begins, beyond the beyond.
Somewhere sweet notes trickle down, no one to tell
Who is there to be the doer and what is done?
Here there is no time or space, no heaven or hell,
Only the One true Being singing an infinite song.
This is the border of the mystery, where I disappear.
This is my home, where I truly belong.

THE SPIRITUAL TREASURE WITHIN

How did we forget our pure, perfect, divine nature? What can we do to return to our original perfection? By making your personal and spiritual growth your first and chief concern, for the welfare of your inner self.

When you consciously explore your spiritual path, you grow in strength, wisdom, and confidence. Inner reflection and spiritual growth are ongoing processes—that take place with or without your awareness. You *can* increase their impact on your life, when you consciously work with them, to the point of making major life decisions from a spiritual perspective. This process of spiritual growth can be very potent. The more you allow your awareness to grow, the more love you embody, the more your being expands.

Being conscious is cutting through your own melodrama. Exist in no mind, be empty, here now and trust that as a situation arises, you will know what is necessary to deal with that situation including the use of your intellect, when appropriate. As you start to flow with the universe and realize that you are a soul that is a part of the Consciousness which runs the Universe, you can face anything—joy, sadness, death—as an opportunity for your growth and awakening. You don't always know how things are going to unfold. But then, you don't really have to.

Being Peaceful

We are innately peaceful beings. Peace is our natural inner state of being, a reflection of the consciousness inside us. We are like a deep lake, peaceful and pure at its core, even if there are disturbances on the surface. Our consciousness is the same—pure, positive, clean, and still—even if we have worries and struggles on the surface of life. Meditation can take us closer in touch with who we really are and toward this inner stillness. Bring your awareness to your body, your breath, and observe your thoughts from a detached perspective.

As you watch the thoughts you generate, you can choose to eliminate all of the ones that steal your peace of mind. Just like we clean out all the dust that settles in our house every day, and throw away all the waste, *removing all the thoughts that steal our joy and peace of mind—through daily meditations—can help clean the dust that settles on our consciousness.*

Can you define what you really mean by peace? When there is no noise, when nobody talks to you, when there is silence, when everything is calm and stands still—is that peace? That's just silence, that allows us to reach that inner stillness and inner quiet we crave so much in our busy lives. The Universe does not require anything to happen outside it, in order that it may be at peace. If that is the truth, then it applies to you also. You require nothing in order to bring you peace of mind. You only require yourself. *There is no need for anything to take place outside, for you to be at peace inside.* Peace does not come from outside. It comes from within.

Contentment is a Decision

Peace and contentment are true yardsticks of our spiritual growth. Contentment is a choice, it's a decision you can make. When you focus on what you have, you come at life from a place of fullness. You attract more abundance into your life. Any sense of lack—of a glass half empty—will attract more of that lackness into your life. You often forget that the things you have in your life right now, are the same things that you were praying for yesterday. Deep inside you might feel grateful for those things. You may even journal about it. Yet, you find that it is still not a *way of being* for you. You still don't embody that gratitude in your interactions. You still go around complaining about the smallest to the largest of things. You have to decide: *Contentment or complaint—which, of the two, is going to be your dominant vibration?*

- Why are you so comfortable voicing a complaint to anyone willing to hear?

- Why, on the other hand, is voicing your appreciation or gratitude such a rare occurrence?

Can you flip this script?

- Can you significantly dial down the part of you that is constantly fault-finding and complaining?

- Can you dial up the number of times you express appreciation?

Each time you genuinely offer gratitude, and appreciate someone or something, you bring pure, positive energy into the experience of the object of your appreciation. Sounds simple. Yet, it is powerful in its pureness.

Contentment is not the fulfillment of what you want, but the realization of what you have.

Contentment is often mistaken for complacency and resignation. Contentment is not about having a passive, laid-back attitude and doing nothing. Contentment is a choice we can actively make. Contentment does not come to those whose means are great, but to those whose needs are few and simple. For me simplicity is at the core of contentment. It's about being content with less, rather than always wanting more, always acquiring more. Examine why you want more. Examine why you are not happy with what you already have while someone else is happy with much less than what you have.

Enough is a decision, not an amount. —Alison Faulkner

Embracing gratitude can be a very powerful game changer as its benefits are both scientific and spiritual. People who regularly practice gratitude experience more positive emotions, feel more alive, sleep better, express more compassion and kindness, and even have stronger immune systems! Gratitude doesn't need to be reserved just for big occasions. You can be grateful for the mattress you sleep on. For the food you just ate. For the friends you can laugh with. For the sunrises and sunsets. For the mountains and the lakes, the trees and the birds. For air and water. For all the victories and the failures. For this *magical experience called life*, on this beautiful planet.

May you notice all the little blessings that fill your life. The ones that often get overlooked because they're always there and you don't need to worry about them. They are stable, consistent and reliable. May you water these little things with your energy and gratitude, so they can become the biggest things in your life. *Just be grateful for the simple miracle of existence, and then see the magic unfold.*

> ***Gratitude is a sacred responsibility affirming your faith in the Divine.***

Gratitude is an affirmation of the goodness in your lives and a spirit of appreciation, showing that you value what you have, from the smallest to the grandest of blessings.

It has been proven scientifically, that writing out a list of things that you are grateful for on a daily basis can significantly increase your well-being and appreciation for life. Many people get excited by this concept and get started. Then some fumble and lose momentum. Consistency is key. Don't give up. When you learn to say thank you first, then you have the right to ask for more from the Universe.

Sometimes you can be grateful for what you have but still not be content, you always want more. All the other spiritual pillars could collapse without the pillar of contentment. Because your ego has taught you to have an endless list of desires, you are conditioned to not be at peace until you check off all the desires. Like checking off items on a grocery list. You *have* to stop postponing your happiness and realize how much you have and be happy and content with what you have now. Because the things you are waiting for may or may not come at all. Then, you would have spent a lifetime being miserable.

All other discussions, intellectual exercises, or debates—about creation and reality, about rebirth and karma, about levels and degrees of realization, about ignorance and enlightenment, about seekers and the sought, are mere mind-froth on the surface of the ocean of our silent being. Peace and contentment are the only two yardsticks of spiritual growth, if you experience these in your life on a regular basis, you know you are on the right path.

Compassion

Buddhism's basic premise is that of compassion, to empathize with the suffering of those around us and take steps to help alleviate their suffering. The Dalai Lama once said, "If you want others to be happy, practice compassion. If you want to be happy, practice compassion."

The sooner you develop compassion on this journey, the sooner you start appreciating that each individual is doing what they must do, there isn't a reason to judge another person or oneself. You merely do what you can, to further your own awakening. — Ramdass

The most compassionate thing you can do for others, is to see them and hear them, fully, in all of their humanness, without judgment, criticism, or attempting to offer them advice. Most times when people show you who they truly are, or open up about their vulnerabilities to you, they are not looking for advice. They are looking for someone to listen to them without judgment and with empathy, compassion, and love.

Being seen fully for who you are, is the most loving thing a person can experience.

It's the biggest gift you can give to others, even when they mess up, even when they aren't perfect. To demonstrate acceptance doesn't necessarily mean that you agree with someone. It means you accept someone out of respect for the dignity of that individual's humanity.

Listening is a sacred skill. Listening is an act of deep compassion.

Listening with our hearts to empathize, rather than listening with our head to defend, is one of the most undervalued relationship skills on the planet. You are being called to learn how to listen. — Ramdass

Imagine feeling compassion for someone even when you are in the middle of an argument with them. Imagine being in their shoes and you will feel that at least half your anger dissipates immediately. Imagine feeling compassion for that customer service representative, who is simply the bearer of bad news if your shipment is delayed or your flight gets canceled. We lose our cool on them so easily without taking a moment to think that there is an actual human being with emotions at the other end. A small moment of compassion from your end toward others, especially in difficult moments such as these, can be so healing and uplifting for both you and the recipient of your benevolence.

Self-compassion is just as important as being compassionate toward others. Sometimes, you might fear that if you show too much compassion to yourself, then you might let yourself off the hook for your mistakes. In reality, compassion has the opposite effect on you. Self-compassion and accountability go hand-in-hand. It makes you want to take more accountability for your shortcomings. It gives you room and energy for self-reflection, instead of using it to reject and resent yourself. Self-compassion also entails acknowledging all the work you are doing on yourself, which is not seen or visible to others. It allows you to understand why something is so challenging for you. Accountability, then, makes you want to think about what steps you can take within your reach, to make life a bit easier for yourself.

Be the reason someone feels welcomed, loved, heard, seen, and supported today.

Surrender is a Sign of Spiritual Trust

What happens when you stop expecting? You start accepting. You learn to Surrender.

Surrender is trust in the deep, unfathomable, infinite intelligence of the Universe. Complete and total acceptance is a conscious choice to drop all forms of resistance to whatever has come in the present moment. Acceptance isn't about liking or approving of something. It is about letting life flow and unfold—without getting in the way. Surrendering to our reality means being willing to work and flow with whatever we have at this moment—instead of fighting it. Surrender is the simple wisdom of accepting, rather than opposing, the flow of life. Surrender is not an act of resignation. It only means you stop resisting what is.

To surrender is to accept what is, without the added judgment or story that it should be going any other way.

When you surrender, you free up a lot of mental and emotional energy. You meet reality with open arms and surrender with grace to what's happening around you. Surrender is the path to experiencing unending peace and entering higher states of consciousness.

The joy of surrender is the wonderful, positive feeling you have when you simply let go. It's stepping out of all limitations, expanding beyond your usual conditioning, and opening to infinite possibilities. There is so little we can control. Thinking that we can force, rush, or push things through our will often takes us far out of balance and pushes the desired outcome further away. When you surrender spiritually, you stop forcing solutions on situations you can't control and, instead, trust that there is a Divine force taking care of everything in a perfectly orchestrated manner. Tremendous life force energy gets released when you surrender like this.

Surrender to the innate and infinite intelligence of the Universe. You will never be misguided.

The single most powerful tool that you have on your spiritual journey—meditation—is also an act of surrender. By turning your awareness away from normal activity and settling to a quieter state of mind, you begin your connection with your inner self.

During meditation, when you slip into the silent spaces between your thoughts, you surrender the small self and all its limitations to your unbounded, eternal Self.

Prayer of Surrender

I allow everything to be what it is. I offer no resistance at all.
I allow everyone to be who they are. I offer no resistance at all.
I surrender the struggle to this infinite and loving presence around me that guides my life.

Rejoice!

Worry, fear, despair and sorrow are all born of the mind.
The rock and the blade of grass,
 the leaf and the caterpillar,
the sunset and the breeze,
the birds flying in effortless harmony against the sky,
the mountains and forests and seas....
everything is perfect, without judgment or comparison or analysis or
interpretation.
What is, is—here and now.
Drop the mind and just be,
like a little child awestruck by the wonder of it all.
When intellect sinks and dissolves
in the simple reality of existence-awareness,
Tranquility and bliss are revealed as divine grace that always is, was
and will be.
Rejoice!
Nothing exists but infinite, joyful peace.

XVII
MERGING INTO CONSCIOUSNESS

What is Consciousness? Consciousness is Pure Love. Consciousness is Awareness. Consciousness is Source Energy. Consciousness is Peace. Consciousness is the Divine Energy that runs the Universe.

Consciousness exists as the tiny, invisible core of every living being, while simultaneously remaining the absolute whole, containing all that exists.

We are all peaceful, eternal beings of consciousness, having a human experience. Consciousness is the higher power, the all-pervading, all-powerful Divine Energy that runs this Universe. This energy is extremely pure, and it vibrates at the level of joy, peace, and pure unconditional love. Think of yourself as a part of this pure Divine Energy that runs this Universe. Consciousness is made of you and you are made of Consciousness. Just like each drop of water is whole in itself, as it is made up of the same ingredients as the entire ocean is.

Since we all come from this Source Energy, we are all inherently ONE. We all come from the same consciousness, we are all One, and we must all journey back into this Oneness.

Many people assume that awareness and consciousness are the same thing. They are not. If we interact with someone, then our mind becomes aware of this person's qualities. That is awareness. Consciousness is not a mental awareness or understanding. Consciousness is an inner state of being. It is something infinitely deeper and more inward than awareness.

We are all born as infinite, eternal, conscious, blissful, pure souls as babies. How, then, do we end up losing our way? As we journey through life, our mind gets contaminated by our conditioning, and our experiences and the ego come in surreptitiously to make our souls impure. But at our very core, we are all pure, peaceful souls who can find true fulfillment only when we go back to being who we truly are, when we go back home, to merge with Source.

Who Are You?

Discover who you really are and put an end to the fear of not knowing.

You are the bridge between light and darkness, heaven and earth.
You are the creator, sustainer, and healer of worlds beyond measure.
You are the first-born child of emptiness and energy, zero and infinity.
You are the eye that Source has become to look upon Herself, and wonder!

Spirituality is a choice in every moment. In every moment, we can make the decision to act with love and move toward Oneness or listen to the voice of our ego and move toward separateness. Since we are all cut from the same cloth of consciousness, when we hurt another, we are only truly hurting ourselves, we are all connected. Nothing happens in an isolated universe.

It is only when we become conscious of Consciousness and connect with Source that we can find pure and lasting happiness. We can operate at lower or higher levels of consciousness or somewhere in between, along the continuum.

People who meditate regularly and connect with that inner stillness and calm are essentially connecting with this pure Consciousness every day. They vibrate higher. Higher consciousness is a state of elevated awareness in which a person has a deeper understanding of reality, the Self and various spiritual aspects of life. This is the best possible state of human evolution, the ultimate perfection, the state of unshakable, eternal peace and joy.

We are all One—beings of Light and Love—sent here to spread unconditional love to everyone around us. Love is all you are, it is your foundation. Buddhism teaches us the values of compassion and that all living beings need to be loved and cherished because Oneness is the only true love, everything else is grasping. If our love is conditional upon people treating us well, or only to our near and dear ones, then our love is not pure love, it is conditional love. We need to purify our minds by developing universal love and compassion to transform this conditional love to pure universal love, that expands to every person and animal on this planet.

All that is required to realize the Self is to be still. What could be easier than that? — Sri Ramana Maharishi

We are very proud of our so-called knowledge. We are inflated by our academic prowess, our degrees and doctorates, our mental libraries, and museums, the books we've read, the seminars and retreats we've attended. We read obscure books and learn all kinds of things. We collect facts and figures, paragraphs and pages, and get into long arguments like we are collecting some great treasure. Yet, we don't get to know our own Self, our own truth, our own soul. The Self is the foundation of all that exists. If you want to make your life worthwhile, seek the truth of the Self in the depths of your heart. Inner energies awaken and divinity takes over. There is nothing else you ever need to know. Meditations can take us closer to this inner stillness to find our Self.

Sink into the silence and the stillness.
Find the root of thought.
Find the source of "I".

Meditation to Connect with Source

- *Drop all earthly concerns for a few moments, all the trappings of the ego and you start to remember again what it's like to simply Be.*

- *Breathe in and breathe out and watch your breath for a few minutes before you keep reading further.*

- *Take your mind beyond the limitations, the turmoil and the fears of this world, to the endless love and peace that lies beyond. Before this moment is nothing. After this moment is nothing. Be completely defenseless, drop all defenses against everyone and everything. Return to your true, natural being. Then all will* _be well._

- _Imagine a shaft of golden light of Divine Energy shining down upon you._

- _Imagine this light filling every part and cell of your body healing all your thoughts, healing your wounds, your fears and reinvigorating every organ, every cell, every muscle in your body._

- _Trust this higher power to heal you of all your worries and wounds completely in this miraculous moment. These are just thoughts and feelings, nothing more._

- _Let go and rely upon your Higher Power for your every need._

- _Begin to feel the energy of oneness as you realize we are all pure souls who all come from Consciousness._

- _You are Awareness itself. Merge into Consciousness._

Enlightenment

Enlightenment is getting lighter—dropping the burden of personality. It is the realization that there is no one who needs to be enlightened.

Direct experience of existence, without distortion by thought, is the key.

Return to innocence, to the state before ego. The state of being is what matters: the doing follows perfectly.

Return to your true, natural being. Then all will be well.

Every human being wants to find true and lasting joy, because this is the very core of our being. Who is it that sees with your eyes, hears with your ears, thinks with your mind, feels with your heart? It's your Self, your soul. The Self is the foundation of all that exists. It is the source and the substance of all things.

Love and peace, truth and bliss, consciousness and wisdom, all are contained in it. Infinite, invisible, omnipotent, imperishable, perfect, without beginning or end. ***The Self is a mystery beyond concept or thought.***

Every living creature lives by the grace of the Self alone. The Self cannot be seen or touched or known, you can only be it. When you have become still and silent; when you have truly gone beyond all attachments and desires; when you have surrendered yourself totally with great love and devotion, then, and only then, the glory of the Self is revealed. You merge forever in that joy, like a river merging with the infinite ocean. At last, your life becomes truly blessed. Joy is a state of being. True and lasting joy does *not* come from objects or people or things. It wells up like a mountain spring from your own inner depths. Turn inwards and find the Source of being, the Heart, the place where the "I" emerges from. This is the greatest discovery you can ever make. It is your birth-right, this inner treasure, an infinite and eternal source of love and joy, strength, light, and peace.

It is the Self, the power behind everything, the center of Divinity. Once you have found it, hold on to it, stay rooted in this perfection. It is yours, always, the greatest gift of all. *This* is the real purpose of your life, the truth of who you really are, the meaning, love and bliss that you have been searching for through thousands of lifetimes. It's right here inside you, right now. So, reverse your attention, go inwards, return to the Source.

All you seek *will* be found.

How Can We Merge with Consciousness?

Less thought, more stillness.
Less talk, more silence.
Less effort, more surrender.
Less me, more everything.

Less ego, more humility.
Less fear, more love.
Less knowledge, more wisdom.
Less doing, more being.

Drop the intellect. Just be.
Thoughtless, desire-less, still.
Dive deep into the silence in your Heart.
Inner energies awaken and take over: let yourself go, surrender and dissolve in the Self.
Find blissful, perfect peace!

Be Still

No name, no face,
No time, no space,
No thought or deed,
No fruit or seed,
No body, no mind,
No forward or behind,
No dream or desire,
No smoke or fire,
No you or me
In stillness, just be:
Perfect peace and clarity.